CREATIVE BAKING

Chiffon Cakes

Susanne Ng

with Tan Phay Shing

Marshall Cavendish Cuisine

The publisher would like to thank Phoon Huat & Co Pte Ltd
and Chew's Group Limited for their support of this publication.

Editor: Lydia Leong
Designer: Adithi Khandadai
All photos by Hongde Photography except step-by-step photos by Susanne Ng and Tan Phay Shing

Published by Marshall Cavendish Cuisine
An imprint of Marshall Cavendish International

Other Marshall Cavendish Offices:
Marshall Cavendish Corporation. 99 White Plains Road, Tarrytown NY 10591-9001, USA •
Marshall Cavendish International (Thailand) Co Ltd. 253 Asoke, 12th Flr, Sukhumvit 21 Road,
Klongtoey Nua, Wattana, Bangkok 10110, Thailand • Marshall Cavendish (Malaysia) Sdn Bhd,
Times Subang, Lot 46, Subang Hi-Tech Industrial Park, Batu Tiga, 40000 Shah Alam,
Selangor Darul Ehsan, Malaysia

Marshall Cavendish is a trademark of Times Publishing Limited

National Library Board, Singapore Cataloguing-in-Publication Data

Names: Ng, Susanne. | Tan, Phay Shing.
Title: Creative baking : chiffon cakes / Susanne Ng, Tan Phay Shing.
Description: Singapore : Marshall Cavendish Cuisine, [2015]
Identifiers: OCN 927056428 | ISBN 978-981-4721-42-4 (paperback)
Subjects: LCSH: Cake | Cookbooks.
Classification: LCC TX771 | DDC 641.8653--dc23

Printed by Markono Print Media Pte Ltd

Dedication

To my husband Guangyou,
our children Caleb, Christine and
Charissa, and my mum and dad

Susanne

To my husband Jianlong,
our children Mun Yew and Mun Zhong,
and my mum and dad

Phay Shing

Contents

Acknowledgements

I would like to thank my husband and best friend for always being by my side, for his understanding and for constantly providing insights into my creations.

I am also grateful to my parents for their unceasing support and love. Without them, I would not have been able to pursue my passion for making creative chiffon cakes.

I am also extremely blessed that my children are ardent supporters of my creations and that even my one-year-old constantly calls out for "cake!"

I will also like to thank my mummy friends (especially those from Christine's group) for their constant support and for starting me on this journey by sharing with me their passion for baking.

Most of all, I would like to thank God for giving me the opportunity and inspiration to bake. He is truly behind every one of my creations.

Susanne

First and foremost, I would like to thank God for providing me with the inspiration and energy to bake while taking care of the kids, cooking for the family and doing the housework. I sometimes wonder how I manage to cope and it could only be with His help.

I am immensely thankful for the support that my husband gives me, whether it is by being my guinea pig for taste testing and giving his brutally honest feedback, providing the kitchen equipment I need, or going out of his way to help me source for natural food colouring products.

I am also thankful that my children are excellent at telling me what looks cute or not, giving me their honest opinions and encouraging me when I encounter failed or difficult bakes.

I am also grateful to my parents for their support and for providing practical help, such as washing up after I bake.

Last but not least, I would like to thank Susanne for inspiring me to start my creative chiffon cake journey, and for generously sharing her experience and insights for baking chiffon cakes. I am truly thankful for her friendship and encouragement.

Phay Shing

6

Together, we would like to thank:

Lydia, our editor for giving us this opportunity to do this book, for her endless patience and support, and for being so accommodating. We could not have asked for a better editor!

Adithi the designer and Hongde the photographer for their professionalism and creativity in making the photography sessions so fun and enjoyable, and making everything look so beautiful!

Phoon Huat & Co Pte Ltd and Chew's Group Limited — our favourite ingredient suppliers — for their kind support of this book.

Introduction

Soft, fluffy, moist, low in sugar and yet flavourful and tasty, chiffon cakes are delicious and healthy treats suitable for people of all ages — and you simply cannot stop eating at one slice!

Chiffon cakes are typically baked in tube pans and look rather standard, but did you know that you can bake chiffon cakes in all sorts of cute and exciting shapes, with all kinds of patterns and in varying sizes as well?

In this book, you will learn how to make cute and creative chiffon cake pops and chiffon cupcakes, from chicks and horses, to watermelons, strawberries and sunflowers, just to name a few! You will also learn how to decorate chiffon cupcakes using healthy chiffon cake instead of sugar-laden fondant.

Within these pages, you will also discover how to make chiffon cakes pretty enough to stand alone as the centrepiece at a party and be the centre of attraction at any gathering! We also show you how to turn chiffon cakes into piñata cakes and hide a surprise in the cake!

We hope you will enjoy recreating these recipes for your loved ones and friends as much as we enjoyed creating them for you.

Susanne & Phay Shing

Basic Tools & Equipment

Chiffon Tube Pans

Chiffon cakes are traditionally baked in tube pans as this type of cake is very delicate and needs to cling to the centre tube and the sides of the pan to enable rising during baking, and prevent sinking while cooling. For this reason, chiffon tube pans must not be greased and non-stick tube pans cannot be used. Standard chiffon tube pan sizes are 15 cm, 18 cm and 23 cm.

When baking single tone chiffon cakes, the capacity is generally:

15-cm chiffon tube pan: 2 egg yolks and 3 egg whites

18-cm chiffon tube pan: 3 egg yolks and 4 egg whites

23-cm chiffon tube pan: 6 egg yolks and 8 egg whites

Dual tone or rainbow chiffon cakes usually require an additional egg or two due to loss while transferring the batter between mixing bowls.

Chiffon tube pans must be inverted during the sensitive stage of cooling so that gravity can help pull the cake to its maximum height before the cake structure stabilizes.

Other Types of Moulds

Through experimenting, we have found that chiffon cakes can be baked in a variety of moulds, provided that the volume is not too large, and the chiffon cake is able to grip on to the surface. Some examples are glass bowls, shaped metal moulds, silicone moulds, paper cones and eggshells.

Moulds with a bigger volume such as glass bowls and metal moulds are preferably inverted during the cooling stage to prevent the cake from sinking. For smaller moulds, inverting does not make a difference to the height of the cooled cake.

To prepare eggshell moulds, make a hole at the narrow end of an egg and drain the contents. Wash the shell thoroughly and peel away the white membrane from the inside of the shell.

In these recipes, we also use shallow baking pans for baking the layer chiffon cakes used in decorating the cakes. The size of the shallow baking pans used will depend on the type of decoration required. When very little decoration is required, the smallest pan size (15-cm x 15-cm) is typically used.

When making roll cakes, the typical baking pan sizes used are 25-cm x 25-cm or 30-cm x 25-cm.

Baking Paper

Also known as parchment or greaseproof paper, baking paper is used to line baking pans when making sheet cakes to enable the cake to be removed easily from the pan. Baking paper should not be used in chiffon tube pans, glass bowls or metal moulds.

Kitchen Scale

As the amount of each ingredient used in making chiffon cakes can be small, and some recipes also call for accuracy down to 1 g, a digital weighing scale is recommended. Digital scales are also preferred for the tare function which enables the scale to discount the weight of the container and only display the weight of the contents. This is useful when the recipe calls for the batter to be divided into a number of portions.

Measuring Spoons

Measuring spoons come in a set: $\frac{1}{8}$ tsp, $\frac{1}{4}$ tsp, $\frac{1}{2}$ tsp, 1 tsp and 1 Tbsp. These spoons can be used for measuring both liquid and dry ingredients. For liquid ingredients, fill the spoon to the brim. For dry ingredients, fill the spoon until it is full, then level it off with a spatula or knife.

Sieve

Sifting dry ingredients such as flour, baking powder or cocoa powder using a fine mesh sieve helps to break up any lumps in the flour and aerate it. This also makes the flour lighter, helping it to be more easily incorporated into the batter, to create a cake that is lighter, finer and more delicate in texture.

Electric Mixer

A handheld electric mixer is recommended for mixing the egg yolk batter, to help incorporate air into the batter. When mixing the egg yolk batter, set the electric mixer to low or medium speed.

For whisking the meringue, both the handheld or stand mixer may be used. The handheld mixer requires high speed to whisk the meringue to firm peaks, so get a handheld mixer with a range of speeds if you are using the same mixer for beating the egg yolks and whisking the egg whites.

Always wash the beater attachment well after mixing the egg yolk batter and ensure it is clean and grease-free before whisking the egg whites, as the presence of grease may affect the foaming properties of the egg whites.

3

6

5

4

7

300W

8 Mixing Bowls

Have a few mixing bowls of various sizes on hand: small ones for the egg yolk batters and larger ones for the egg whites where the meringue increases many times in volume. The mixing bowl for the meringue must be grease-free and cannot be made from plastic. Metal and glass mixing bowls are recommended for use with the meringue.

9 Pastry Brush

Keep small parts of the cake moist by brushing with a sugar syrup, especially for designs where the assembly requires more time.

10 Silicone Spatula and Silicone Whisk

Folding the meringue into the egg yolk batter requires very gentle mixing, and a flexible silicone spatula or silicone whisk is recommended in combination with gentle unidirectional strokes.

11 Pastry Scraper

This is used to level the batter in the baking pan when baking sheet cakes to ensure the cake is of an even thickness.

12 Cookie Cutters or Plunger Cutters

Cutters in various shapes such as circles, hearts, flowers and stars are used to cut out shapes from the sheet cakes for simple decorations.

13 Oven Thermometer

This is an important tool for monitoring the oven temperature since chiffon cakes are extremely sensitive to changes in temperature, and especially since many recipes call for sequential reduction in temperature and not all ovens may respond similarly. For example, my small oven takes 2 minutes longer to adjust to the temperature change compared to my larger oven. Hence it is extremely important to check for doneness using a skewer.

14 Piping Tips and Piping Bags

2 mm to 3 mm rounded tips are typically used for piping patterns when making decorated chiffon cakes. If you do not have piping tips, improvise by cutting a 2 mm or 3 mm hole at the tip of a disposable piping bag.

Basic Ingredients

DRY INGREDIENTS

Cake Flour

In baking chiffon cakes, cake flour is used instead of plain (all-purpose) flour as it has a low protein content and will yield cakes with a softer, finer texture and a more tender crumb. It is also important to sift the cake flour before use to aerate it and remove any lumps in the flour. Sifting will also allows the flour to be more easily mixed into the batter, ensuring that the batter is not over mixed.

Sugar

Castor sugar is used in the egg yolk batter and meringue in all the recipes in this book. Castor sugar is finer than regular granulated sugar, and will dissolve more quickly. This is especially useful when whisking meringues. Castor sugar is not to be confused with icing or confectioner's sugar, which is ground into powder and sometimes mixed with cornstarch to prevent clumping. Do not use regular granulated sugar or icing sugar in place of castor sugar in these recipes as the texture of the cake will be affected.

Cream of Tartar

Cream of tartar is used for stabilising egg whites when whisking the meringue. It also helps to increase the heat tolerance and volume of meringue. Cream of tartar is essentially potassium bitartrate, made from tartaric acid which stabilises the meringue. Generally, only $1/16$ tsp or a pinch of cream of tartar is needed per egg white in making chiffon cakes. Too much cream of tartar will result in the cake tasting sour. Cream of tartar can also be substituted with lemon juice or white vinegar. Replace every $1/2$ tsp cream of tartar with 1 tsp lemon juice or white vinegar.

Baking Powder

Baking powder is usually omitted and not necessary for light and fluffy chiffon cakes if the meringue is correctly whisked and folded. However, there are certain exceptions, such as when a recipe calls for a substantial amount of citrus zest, cocoa powder or red yeast powder, all which have the effect of dampening the batter. We also use baking powder in recipes that call for dense liquid ingredients such as pumpkin purée and honey.

Cocoa Powder

There are two types of cocoa powder: natural and Dutch-processed (or alkalised) cocoa powder. Dutch-processed cocoa powder is used in all the recipes in this book and for ease, we will refer to it as cocoa powder.

Both natural and Dutch-processed cocoa powder are made from cocoa beans, but Dutch-processed cocoa beans are soaked in an alkaline solution before being dried, which lowers their acidity, resulting in a darker colour, and also less harsh and richer chocolate flavour. Both types of cocoa powder are commonly used in baking, but when natural cocoa powder is used, baking soda is usually required for the leavening action with the acid which helps the cake rise and also prevent the formation of big holes in chiffon cakes. When Dutch-processed cocoa powder is used, only baking powder is required.

Salt

Only a pinch of salt is required in these chiffon cake recipes to help perk up the other flavours in the cake and also to offset the sweetness of the cake.

WET INGREDIENTS

Eggs

Medium eggs weighing on average 65 g (with shell) are used in all the recipes in this book.

Chiffon cakes require the egg yolks and egg whites to be separated. Cold eggs separate more easily, but eggs whip to a higher volume when at room temperature. If preferred, you can separate the eggs when cold, then set them aside for 10–15 minutes to warm to room temperature.

When separating the egg yolk from the egg white, use a separate bowl to avoid getting any egg yolk in the lot of egg whites should the egg yolk break. The presence of egg yolk may affect the foaming properties of the egg white.

Egg whites from fresh eggs (less than 4 days old) are important for whipping up beautiful and stable meringues for chiffon cakes. Egg whites from older eggs are thinner and form less stable meringues as the liquid can separate more easily. Storing the eggs in a cool place will help to keep them fresh for longer.

8   Oil

We use vegetable or corn oil, but any light or mild tasting vegetable oil is suitable for use in these recipes. Oil is used in chiffon cakes to give the cakes a lighter, more airy texture compared to cakes made using butter. In our experience, there are no significant differences in taste and texture from using vegetable or corn oil.

9   Liquid (Water/Fruit Purée/Juice/Milk/Coconut Milk/Yoghurt)

The liquid content of chiffon cakes is typically made up of ingredients such as water, fruit purées, juices, milk or yoghurt, in addition to oil. As a higher liquid to flour ratio will yield a softer albeit less stable chiffon cake, we have optimised the ratio in these recipes to obtain the softest texture possible. Thus, it is essential that the measurements are taken accurately to ensure the cake turns out successfully.

10   Extract and Flavouring

Extracts and flavourings such as vanilla extract, strawberry paste and pandan paste etc. are used in small amounts in these recipes to enhance the flavour of the cake. They are typically packaged in small bottles and are available from baking supply stores as well as some supermarkets.

Zest from citrus fruit such as oranges and lemons is used in some recipes to flavour the cakes. The zest is obtained by grating the thin, coloured outer layer of the citrus fruit. Avoid grating the white layer under the zest as it is bitter. Like extracts and flavourings, zest helps to enhance flavour and taste in baking.

11   Food Colouring

We try to use natural food colouring such as cocoa powder, charcoal powder, red yeast powder and matcha powder as much as possible in our baking, although synthetic food colouring produces more vibrant colours.

Food colouring comes in gel and liquid forms. We prefer gel food colouring as the colour is more concentrated and only a touch is required. To add colouring, dip the tip of a toothpick or skewer into the food colouring, then into the egg yolk batter. Adjust the intensity of the colour as desired. Note that the colour will lighten when the meringue is added to the egg yolk batter.

Basic Recipes & Techniques

Making a chiffon cake

Egg Yolk Batter

Egg yolks

Castor sugar

Vegetable/corn oil

Water/fruit purée/juice/
   milk/yoghurt

Vanilla extract/flavouring

Cake flour, sifted

Cocoa powder, sifted

Baking powder, sifted

Salt

Meringue

Egg whites

Cream of tartar

Castor sugar

Note Many chiffon cake recipes call for the same number of egg yolks and egg whites. However, we have found that using more egg whites result in lighter, fluffier chiffon cakes.

1. Prepare egg yolk batter. Using an electric mixer at medium speed, beat egg yolks and sugar in a mixing bowl until pale in colour.

2. Add oil, water/fruit purée/juice/milk/yoghurt and vanilla extract/flavouring. Mix well and set aside.

3. In another bowl, sift together any powdered ingredients such as flour, cocoa powder and baking powder.

4. Add sifted ingredients and salt to egg yolk batter. Mix until no trace of flour is found. Set aside.

5. Prepare meringue. In a clean, grease-free mixing bowl, whisk egg whites with cream of tartar at high speed until foamy.

6. Add half the sugar and whisk at high speed until soft peaks form.

7. Add remaining sugar and continue to whisk at high speed until firm peaks form.

8. Using a spatula, gently fold meringue into egg yolk batter one-third at a time.

9. Pour batter into desired mould. If baking in a baking pan, level batter with a pastry scraper. Gently tap mould on counter top to release any air bubbles.

10. Bake as instructed in recipe until top of cake springs back slightly when lightly pressed with a finger and a skewer inserted into the centre of cake comes out clean. Remove from oven.

11. If cake is baked in a tube pan, invert pan on a wire rack once out of the oven and set aside to cool completely before unmoulding. This is to ensure that the delicate cake does not collapse on its own weight while cooling. Cooling may take up to 2 hours.

12. Some bakers prefer to shock the cake by dropping it still in the pan, when it is fresh out of the oven, from a height of about 10 cm, before leaving to cool upright. This shock treatment is thought to prevent shrinkage.

1
2
4
5
6
7
8
9

Unmoulding chiffon cakes from tube pans

1. To unmould, gently pull cake from sides of tube pan, turning tube pan as you go to loosen sides of cake.

2. Lift removable base up to unmould sides.

3. Gently lift cake from base using one hand, turning cake as you go, to loosen base of cake.

4. Invert cake. Lift and remove base of tube pan to release cake.

Scan the QR code to view a video tutorial on unmoulding chiffon cakes from tube pans.

Unmoulding chiffon cakes from glass or metal moulds, paper cones and eggshells

Glass or Metal Mould: Pull cake away from sides of mould to loosen cake, then invert mould to release cake.

Paper Cone: Unmould by peeling paper cone from narrow end, following sealed edge of paper cone to ensure tip of cake does not break off.

Eggshell: Unmould by gently cracking the eggshell all around the cake using the back of a metal spoon, then peeling off the shell in small pieces.

Glass or metal mould

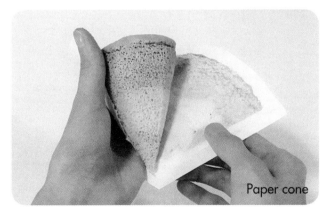

Paper cone

Eggshell

Making marshmallow cream

1. To adhere cake to cake, marshmallow cream is used.

2. To make, place 3–4 white marshmallows in a microwave-safe bowl and sprinkle with a little water. Heat in the microwave oven on High for 30 seconds, then remove and stir until smooth.

3. If mixture is too dry, add a few drops of hot water and stir. If too watery, add 1–2 marshmallows and repeat heating process.

4. Alternatively, melt marshmallows with a sprinkle of water in a double boiler and stir.

Making syrup

1. Small parts of the cake can be kept moist by brushing with syrup.

2. Syrup can be made in a 1:2 ratio or 1:3 ratio of sugar to water depending on how sweet or thick you prefer it to be.

3. Dissolve 10 g sugar in 20–30 g hot water. Stir well and set aside to cool.

Making pandan juice

1. Pandan juice will add a light fragrance and green tinge to cakes.

2. Prepare fresh pandan juice by blending 10–15 fresh pandan leaves (tips trimmed and cut into small pieces) with 50 g water.

3. Strain with a sieve and extract all the liquid. Discard pulp.

Making blue colouring from blue pea flowers

1. Cakes can be naturally coloured using strawberry purée, pumpkin purée, blueberry powder, pandan juice, charcoal powder and cocoa powder, but the colours may not be as vivid as using food colouring.

2. To make a natural blue colouring, place about 35 dried blue pea flowers in a small bowl with 10 g hot water. Ensure flowers are fully submerged. Let soak for 15–30 minutes, then strain liquid into another bowl, squeezing flowers to extract all the liquid. Discard pulp.

Chiffon Cake 101

Ensure quality of meringue

The quality of the meringue is extremely important in ensuring that the resulting chiffon cake is soft and fluffy, and does not collapse upon cooling.

An under beaten meringue (soft peaks) will result in a very dense cake and an over beaten meringue (overly stiff and dry peaks) will cause the cake to crack open or explode its top, and also have a texture that is not as fine or tender.

The perfect meringue should have firm peaks or just reach stiff peaks (but not beyond) and stick to the bowl when you overturn the bowl.

Use fresh eggs

A perfect meringue is the result not only of applying the correct technique of beating, but also of using fresh eggs. Store eggs in a cool, dry place to maximise shelf life.

Use light and gentle strokes

Add the meringue to the egg yolk batter in 3 additions and fold gently and lightly in the same direction, just to the point of uniform incorporation. Do not over fold as over folding will cause the baked cake to have a very dense texture.

Baking temperature and timing

The optimal baking temperatures and timings are listed in the recipes, but as individual oven temperatures and conditions vary, it is best to use an oven thermometer to check the temperature of your oven and use a skewer to test the baked cakes for doneness.

Prevent drying out

Always keep chiffon cakes well wrapped up or in airtight containers to prevent them from drying out. Brush syrup on any small parts if you are not going to use them right away.

Storing chiffon cakes

Stored in airtight containers, chiffon cakes will keep for up to 2 days at room temperature or up to 5 days refrigerated.

Troubleshooting Guide

Cake falls out of pan

The chiffon cake falls out of the pan
when it is inverted for cooling and starts to shrink.

The chiffon cake is likely to be under baked.
Try increasing the baking time by intervals of 5 minutes.

Cake caves in

The top of the chiffon cake has caved in
after it is cooled and removed from the mould.

The liquid to flour ratio was wrong, causing the cake to be heavy
and pulled down while it was inverted. Ensure that all ingredients
are measured correctly and accurately.

Cake has exploded top

Chiffon cake has an overly exploded top
causing the cake to have a wide base when inverted.

The meringue may have been over beaten and
too stiff, or the chiffon pan was filled too full.
The perfect meringue should be firm and glossy.
When filling the chiffon pan, leave a minimum
2-cm gap from the rim of the pan.

Cake has large air pockets

Chiffon cake has large air pockets.

Before placing the pan into the oven to bake, tap it
gently on the counter top to release any air bubbles.
If the air pockets are uneven and there are specks
of white in the pockets, the meringue may not have
been folded in completely or uniformly.

Cake cracks

Chiffon cake has cracks on top once out of the oven.

Fret not! Small cracks are normal and will not be seen once
the cake is inverted. If the cracks are large, you may have
overfilled the mould. When filling a mould with batter, leave
a minimum 2-cm gap from the rim of the mould. If preferred,
steam baking may help to eliminate cracks. To steam bake,
place a pan of water under the lowest rack in the oven
to create steam while the cake bakes.

Cake browns

Chiffon cake browns, hiding the colour/pattern.

Try reducing the oven temperature by 10°C each time
until you get the right temperature for baking these
coloured chiffon cakes your oven,
since individual ovens may work differently.

Little Bites
of Fun!

Strawberry Yoghurt Watermelon Cake Pops

Makes 9–10 cake pops

Egg yolk batter

3 egg yolks

25 g castor sugar

40 g vegetable/corn oil

40 g strawberry yoghurt drink

$\frac{1}{2}$ tsp vanilla extract

60 g cake flour, sifted

A pinch of salt, sifted

$\frac{1}{2}$ tsp pandan paste

1 tsp strawberry paste

Meringue

4 egg whites

$\frac{1}{4}$ tsp cream of tartar

45 g castor sugar

Finishing

Raisins, as needed

Marshmallow cream (page 24)

1. Prepare 9–10 paper cones and about 2 deep baking pans for holding paper cones. To make paper cone holder, wrap each baking pan with at least 2 layers of aluminium foil, then use a chopstick to make about 6 holes, spacing them apart, to allow paper cones to stand upright. Gently insert paper cones into holes, widening holes as necessary.

2. Preheat oven to 160°C.

3. Prepare egg yolk batter (page 20). Spoon 13 tsp batter into a small bowl. Add pandan paste and mix well. Add strawberry paste to remaining batter and mix well.

4. Prepare meringue (page 20). Gently fold meringue one-third at a time into respective egg yolk batters: 26 Tbsp (1$\frac{2}{3}$ cups) meringue into pandan batter and the rest into strawberry batter.

5. Fill cones with strawberry batter until half full. Top with a layer of pandan batter.

6. Bake at 160°C for 15 minutes, then 150°C for 10–15 minutes, or until a skewer inserted into the centre of cakes comes out clean.

7. Place pan of cones on a wire rack to cool completely before unmoulding.

8. Slice raisins for watermelon seeds and adhere to cake using marshmallow cream).

Rainbow Cake Pops

Makes 12 cake pops

Egg yolk batter

3 egg yolks

25 g castor sugar

50 g vegetable/corn oil

50 g water/fresh milk

$^1/_2$ tsp vanilla extract

80 g cake flour, sifted

A pinch of salt

Pink, yellow, blue, green and
  purple gel food colouring

Meringue

4 egg whites

$^1/_4$ tsp cream of tartar

45 g castor sugar

Note The amount of batter needed to fill a paper cone is approximately twice that needed for the eggshells, so you can vary the number of cone- or egg-shaped cake pops as desired.

1. Prepare 6 paper cones and 6 eggshells, and baking pans as needed for holding cones and eggshells (page 33). Preheat oven to 160°C.

2. Prepare egg yolk batter (page 20). Divide batter into 5 portions and place into separate bowls: 5 tsp for red, 5 tsp for yellow, 6 tsp for green, 6 tsp for blue and 7 tsp for purple. Add a drop of food colouring to each bowl and mix thoroughly.

3. Prepare meringue (page 20). Gently fold meringue one-third at a time into respective egg yolk batters: 10 Tbsp meringue into red batter, 10 Tbsp meringue into yellow batter, 12 Tbsp meringue into green batter, 12 Tbsp meringue into blue batter and 14 Tbsp meringue into purple batter.

4. Use a teaspoon to spoon colours layer by layer into cones and eggshells.

5. Bake at 160°C for 10 minutes, then 150°C for 10–15 minutes or until a skewer inserted into the centre of cakes comes out clean.

6. Place pans on a wire rack to cool completely before unmoulding.

7. Insert a cake pop stick into each cake.

Orange-Cocoa Horse Cake Pops

Makes 16 cake pops

Egg yolk batter

2 egg yolks

10 g castor sugar

28 g vegetable/corn oil

28 g orange juice

40 g cake flour, sifted

A pinch of salt

1 tsp finely grated orange zest

1/4 tsp orange emulco (optional)

1/3 tsp cocoa powder, sifted

Meringue

3 egg whites

1/5 tsp cream of tartar

35 g castor sugar

Finishing

Compound milk chocolate
or dark chocolate, melted

Chocolate-coated biscuit sticks

Note The baking time may vary according to size of the eggshells used. Test that the cakes are done using a skewer.

---

1. Prepare 16 eggshells and baking pans as needed for holding eggshells (page 33). Preheat oven to 160°C.

2. Prepare egg yolk batter (page 20). Divide batter into 2 equal portions. Add orange zest and orange emulco to one portion and cocoa powder to the other. Mix well.

3. Prepare meringue (page 20). Divide meringue into 2 equal portions and fold gently and quickly in 3 additions into orange and cocoa batters.

4. Fill 8 eggshells with 1 1/2 tsp orange batter and the other 8 with 1 1/2 tsp cocoa batter to form muzzle of horse. Top eggshells with a different batter until two-thirds full to form rest of head.

5. Bake at 160°C for 5 minutes, then 150°C for 10 minutes and 140°C for 5–10 minutes or until a skewer inserted into the centre of cakes comes out clean. Set aside to cool completely before unmoulding.

6. With a small serrated knife and sawing motion, gently cut off the rough top portion of cakes at opening of eggshell.

7. Cut a small rectangular block from the top to create ears.

8. Spoon melted chocolate into a piping bag and make a small hole at the tip. Draw horses' mane, eyes and nostrils using melted chocolate or use a toothpick to paint features on. Let chocolate set completely.

9. Use a toothpick or skewer to make a hole at the base of each cake. Insert a chocolate coated biscuit stick into the hole when ready to serve to prevent biscuits from softening.

Strawberry Yoghurt Strawberry Cake Pops

Makes 18 cake pops

Egg yolk batter

2 egg yolks

15 g castor sugar

28 g vegetable/corn oil

14 g strawberry purée

14 g strawberry yoghurt

40 g cake flour, sifted

A pinch of salt, sifted

1/2 tsp pandan paste

Green and red gel food colouring

1/2 tsp strawberry paste

1/4 tsp red yeast powder, sifted

Meringue

3 egg whites

1/5 tsp cream of tartar

35 g castor sugar

Finishing

Marshmallow cream (page 24)

2 tsp cocoa powder

1 1/2 tsp hot water

1. Position baking rack to second lowest position. Preheat oven to 160°C. Line two 15-cm square baking pans with baking paper. Prepare 18 eggshells and baking pans as needed for holding eggshells (page 33).

2. Prepare egg yolk batter (page 20). Spoon one-third of batter into another bowl. Add pandan paste and 2–3 drops of green colouring and mix well. To remaining batter, add strawberry paste, red yeast powder and 2–3 drops of red colouring. Mix well.

3. Prepare meringue (page 20). Gently fold meringue one-third at a time into respective egg yolk batters: one-third of meringue into green batter and remaining meringue into red batter.

4. Pour green batter into square pans and gently tap on counter top to release any air bubbles. Fill each eggshell with 2 heaping teaspoonfuls of red batter.

5. Bake sheet cakes at 160°C for 10 minutes and eggshell cakes at 160°C for 10 minutes, followed by 140°C for 5–7 minutes, or until a skewer inserted into the centre of cakes comes out clean.

6. Invert sheet cakes on baking paper and let cool. Allow cakes in eggshells to cool completely before unmoulding.

7. Pinch one end of red cakes to create strawberry shape.

8. Peel baking paper from green sheet cake and place on a cutting mat. Use a calix shaped cutter or star cookie cutter to cut out leaves. Adhere leaves to strawberries using marshmallow cream.

9. Mix cocoa powder with hot water to form a paste with the consistency of melted chocolate. Add more or less water as needed, a few drops at a time.

10. Transfer chocolate paste to a piping bag and cut a small hole at the tip. Pipe dots for strawberry seeds on cakes.

Pandan Christmas Tree Cake Pops

Makes 9 cake pops

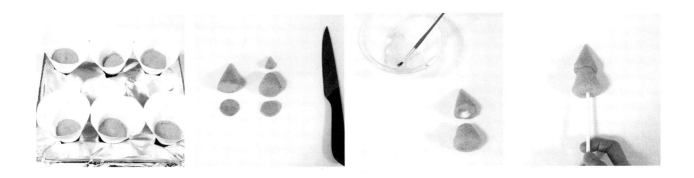

Egg yolk batter

2 egg yolks

16 g castor sugar

26 g vegetable/corn oil

28 g coconut milk/fresh milk

$1/2$ tsp vanilla extract

60 g cake flour, sifted

A pinch of salt

1 tsp pandan paste

Meringue

3 egg whites

$1/4$ tsp cream of tartar

30 g castor sugar

Finishing

Dragée

Marshmallow cream (page 24)

Icing sugar

1. Prepare 18 paper cones and baking pans as needed for holding paper cones (page 33).

2. Preheat oven to 160°C.

3. Prepare egg yolk batter (page 20). Add pandan paste to make green batter.

4. Prepare meringue (page 20). Gently fold meringue into egg yolk batter one-third at a time.

5. Use a teaspoon to fill cones with green batter until about 4-cm deep.

6. Bake at 160°C for 10 minutes, then 150°C for 15 minutes or until a skewer inserted into the centre of cakes comes out clean.

7. Place pan of cones on a wire rack to cool completely before unmoulding.

8. Trim base of cones to level them. Slice off apex (about 1 cm) of 9 cones for bottom layer of trees. Join cakes using marshmallow cream.

9. Insert a cake pop stick into the base of each tree.

10. Decorate with dragée using marshmallow cream. Dust with icing sugar, if desired.

Vanilla-Chocolate Ice Cream Cake Pops

Makes 6 cake pops

Egg yolk batter

4 egg yolks

27 g castor sugar

53 g vegetable/corn oil

53 g water

1 tsp vanilla extract

80 g cake flour, sifted

A pinch of salt

30 g raisins, or more if preferred

2 Tbsp cocoa powder, sifted

Meringue

5 egg whites

1/4 tsp cream of tartar

60 g castor sugar

Finishing

Marshmallow cream (page 24)

1. Prepare 6 glass bowls, each about 8.5-cm wide, and 6 paper cones. Prepare baking pan for holding paper cones (page 33).

2. Preheat oven to 160°C.

3. Prepare egg yolk batter (page 20). Spoon 22 tsp (7 1/3 Tbsp) batter into another bowl and add raisins. Mix well. Add cocoa powder to remaining batter and mix well.

4. Prepare meringue (page 20). Spoon 44 Tbsp (2 3/4 cups) meringue into another bowl and gently fold into raisin batter one-third at a time. Repeat to fold remaining meringue into cocoa batter one-third at a time.

5. Spoon raisin batter equally into glass bowls until bowls are about two-thirds full. Spoon cocoa batter into paper cones until cones are about three-quarters full. Gently tap bowls and cones on counter top to release any air bubbles.

6. Bake at 160°C for 15 minutes, then 150°C for 10–15 minutes, or until a skewer inserted into the centre of cakes comes out clean.

7. Place bowls and pan of cones on a wire rack to cool completely before unmoulding.

8. Assemble parts using marshmallow cream.

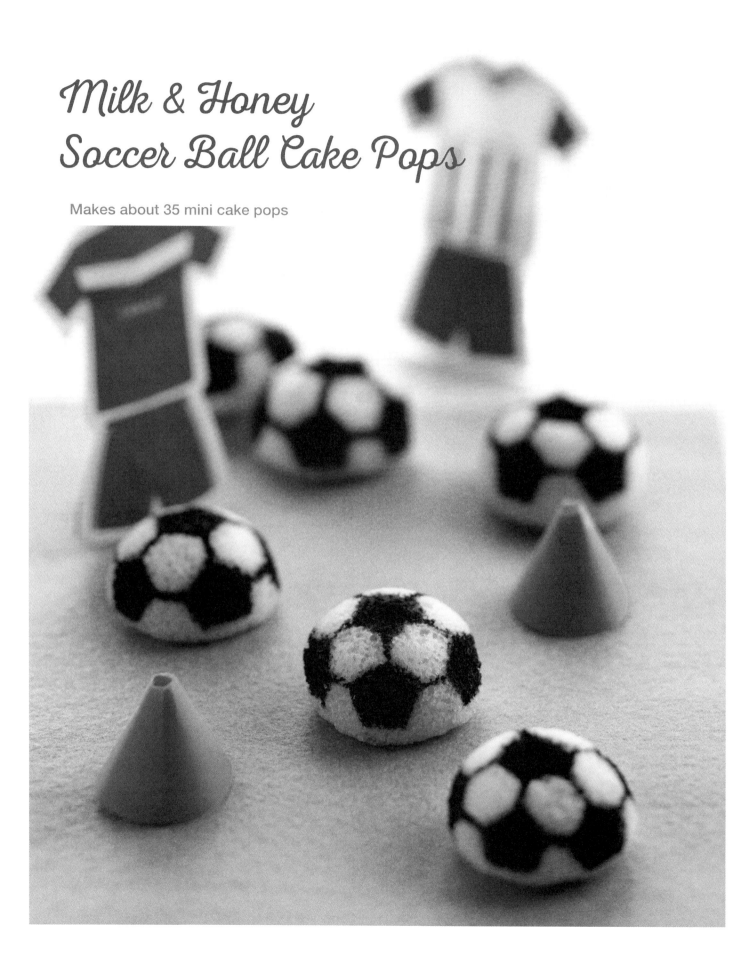

Milk & Honey
Soccer Ball Cake Pops

Makes about 35 mini cake pops

Egg yolk batter

2 egg yolks

10 g castor sugar

28 g vegetable/corn oil

28 g fresh milk, warmed and
  mixed with $1/2$ Tbsp (10 g) honey

1 tsp vanilla extract

45 g cake flour, sifted

$1/4$ tsp baking powder, sifted

A pinch of salt

Meringue

3 egg whites

$1/5$ tsp cream of tartar

30 g sugar

Finishing

2-cm thick slice of carrot

$1/2$ tsp charcoal powder

$1/2$ tsp cocoa powder

1 tsp hot water

1. Position baking rack to second lowest position. Preheat oven to 150°C. Very lightly grease a silicone cake pop mould with oil.

2. Prepare egg yolk batter (page 20) and meringue (page 20).

3. Gently fold meringue into egg yolk batter one-third at a time. Spoon batter into cake pop mould until cavities are almost full.

4. Bake at 150°C for 10 minutes, then 140°C for 5 minutes or until a skewer inserted into cake pops comes out clean. Carefully unmould cake pops.

5. Make stamp for decorating cake pops. Cut carrot into a pentagon, each side about 7 mm long.

6. Mix charcoal and cocoa powders with hot water.

7. Brush stamp with charcoal-cocoa mixture, dab off any excess on a paper towel and make a print in the middle of each cake pop. Paint thin lines extending out of each corner of pentagon and stamp pentagon shapes at the end of each line. Join ring of pentagons with a horizontal line to look like a soccer ball. Fill in pentagons with charcoal-cocoa mixture to enhance print. Let charcoal-cocoa mixture air-dry for about 10 minutes.

Strawberry-Vanilla Mushroom Cake Pops

Makes 10 cake pops

Egg yolk batter

2 egg yolks

14 g castor sugar

26 g vegetable/corn oil

24 g water

1 tsp vanilla extract

40 g cake flour, sifted

A pinch of salt

2 g red yeast powder, sifted

¼ tsp strawberry paste

Meringue

3 egg white

¼ tsp cream of tartar

20 g castor sugar

Finishing

Marshmallow cream (page 24)

1. Preheat oven to 160°C. Prepare a silicone cake pop mould. Line a 15-cm square baking pan and a 10-cm baking pan.

2. Prepare egg yolk batter (page 20) and pour half into another bowl. To one portion, add red yeast powder and strawberry paste. Mix well.

3. Prepare meringue (page 20). Spoon half the meringue (about 20 Tbsp) into another bowl and gently fold into strawberry batter one-third at a time. Repeat to fold remaining meringue into plain batter one-third at a time.

4. Spoon strawberry batter equally into 6 cavities in cake pop mould and bake at 160°C for 12 minutes. Leave cake pop mould to cool on a wire rack before unmoulding.

5. Spoon plain batter into prepared 15-cm pan until batter is about 2-cm deep, then pour remaining batter into 10-cm pan to create a thin sheet. Gently tap pans on counter top to release any air bubbles.

6. Bake 15-cm pan at 160°C for 18 minutes and 10-cm pan at 160°C for 14 minutes.

7. Invert cakes onto a sheet of baking paper and let cool.

8. Peel baking paper from plain sheet cakes and place on a cutting mat. Use a small round cutter to cut out 18–24 small rounds from thin sheet for spots on mushrooms. Use a larger round cutter to cut out 6 rounds from thick sheet cake for mushroom stems.

9. Place 3 or 4 spots on each red mushroom cap and adhere with marshmallow cream. Adhere stems to mushroom caps with marshmallow cream.

Orange Hatching Chick Cupcakes

Makes five 11-mm cakes

Egg yolk batter

3 egg yolks

20 g castor sugar

40 g vegetable/corn oil

43 g orange juice

1 tsp finely grated orange zest

60 g cake flour, sifted

A pinch of salt

Black and yellow
  gel food colouring

1/4 tsp orange emulco

Meringue

4 egg whites

1/4 tsp cream of tartar

45 g sugar

Finishing

Marshmallow cream (page 24)

Note The eyes, beaks and feet can also be drawn on using melted chocolate or food marker. But do this only on the day of serving to prevent smudging.

---

1. Preheat oven to 160°C. Prepare five 11-mm round glass bowls and a 15-cm square baking pan. Line pan with baking paper.

2. Prepare egg yolk batter (page 20). Spoon 14 tsp batter into another bowl and leave plain. Spoon 3 tsp batter each into 2 small bowls. Add a little yellow colouring to one bowl and black to the other. Mix well. Add orange emulco to remaining batter.

3. Prepare meringue (page 20). Gently fold meringue one-third at a time into respective egg yolk batters: 28 Tbsp (1³/₄ cups) meringue into plain batter, 6 Tbsp meringue each into yellow and black batters, and remaining meringue into orange batter.

4. Spoon some plain and orange batters into separate piping bags and make a small hole at the tips. Using plain batter, pipe a zigzag line in each glass bowl for broken eggshell. Bake zigzag line for 1¹/₂ minutes at 160°C.

5. Pipe more plain batter to fill eggshell and other side with some orange batter for chick before topping both sides with remaining plain and orange batters until batter is about 1.5 cm from rim.

6. Gently tap bowls on counter top to release any air bubbles. Bake at 160°C for 10 minutes, then 150°C for 15–17 minutes, or until a skewer inserted into centre of cakes comes out clean. Invert bowls on a wire rack to cool completely before unmoulding.

7. Prepare sheet cake. Pour yellow and black batters side by side into baking pan. Bake at 160°C for 14 minutes. Invert sheet cake onto a sheet of baking paper and let cool.

8. Peel baking paper from sheet cake and place on a cutting mat. From black sheet cake, use a straw to punch out 10 circles for eyes. From yellow sheet cake, use a square cutter to cut out 3 squares, then cut into triangles for beaks; use a star cutter to cut out 10 stars and slice off 2 pointed ends from each star to form feet. Assemble parts using marshmallow cream.

Rainbow Heart Cupcakes

Makes six 8.5-cm cakes

Egg yolk batter

1 egg yolk

10 g castor sugar

40 g vegetable/corn oil

38 g water

1 tsp vanilla extract

60 g cake flour, sifted +
 $\frac{1}{4}$ tsp for thickening red batter

A pinch of salt

Red, orange, yellow, green, blue
 and purple gel food colouring

Meringue

4 egg whites

$\frac{1}{4}$ tsp cream of tartar

50 g castor sugar

1. Preheat oven to 160°C. Prepare six 8.5-cm round glass bowls.

2. Prepare egg yolk batter (page 20). Divide batter into 6 portions and place into separate bowls: 1 tsp for red, 4 tsp for orange, 5 tsp for yellow, 6 tsp for green, 7 tsp for blue and 8 tsp for purple. Add a drop of food colouring to each bowl and mix thoroughly. Note that the colour will lighten when the meringue is added.

3. Add $\frac{1}{4}$ tsp sifted cake flour to red batter and mix well.

4. Prepare meringue (page 20). Fold 3 Tbsp meringue into red batter in 2 additions. Transfer batter into a piping bag fitted with a 2-mm round tip or cut a 2-mm hole at the tip.

5. Draw a heart on a sheet of paper and place under glass bowl as a template. Use red batter to trace and colour in heart on base of bowl. Repeat for all bowls. If using metal moulds, trace hearts on base of moulds using edible marker or pipe freehand.

6. Bake at 160°C for 3–4 minutes if using glass bowls and $1\frac{1}{2}$-2 minutes if using metal moulds.

7. Fold remaining meringue into rest of coloured batters in 2 additions: 8 Tbsp meringue into orange batter, 10 Tbsp meringue into yellow batter, 12 Tbsp meringue into green batter, 14 Tbsp meringue into blue batter and 16 Tbsp meringue into purple batter.

8. Transfer batters into individual piping bags fitted with 6-mm round tips or make a 6-mm hole at the tips. Pipe batter in concentric circles in each bowl. Start with orange, followed by yellow, green, blue and purple.

9. Bake at 160°C for 10 minutes, then 140°C for 20–25 minutes or until a skewer inserted into the centre of cakes comes out clean.

10. Invert cakes on a wire rack to cool completely before unmoulding.

Pandan Ogura Frog Cupcakes

Makes three 10-cm cakes

Egg yolk batter

3 egg yolks + $^{1}/_{2}$ whole egg

32.5 g corn oil

30 g coconut milk

2 tsp pandan juice (page 25)

32.5 g cake flour, sifted + more for thickening coloured batters

$^{1}/_{4}$ tsp salt

1 tsp cocoa powder, sifted

Pink gel food colouring

Meringue

3 egg whites

$^{1}/_{5}$ tsp cream of tartar

37.5 g castor sugar

Finishing

Marshmallow cream (page 24)

> *Note* Ogura cakes are similar to chiffon cakes except that they have a slightly lower flour content and whole egg is used in the egg yolk batter. The cake is then baked in steam.

1. Preheat oven to 150°C. Place a pan of water under the lowest rack in the oven for steam baking. Prepare three 10-cm oval glass bowls. Line two 15-cm square baking pans with baking paper.

2. Prepare egg yolk batter (page 20) with egg yolks and whole egg. Spoon 4 tsp batter into another bowl and add cocoa powder. Spoon 2 tsp batter into another bowl and add a small drop of pink colouring. Add $^{1}/_{3}$ tsp cake flour to each batter and mix well.

3. Prepare meringue (page 20). For ogura cakes, the meringue is beaten until just before firm peaks form. Spoon 8 Tbsp meringue into brown batter, 4 Tbsp into pink batter and remainder into pandan batter. Fold in gently and quickly.

4. Transfer brown and pink batters into separate piping bags fitted with 2-mm round tips or cut a 2-mm hole at the tips. Pipe a mouth in brown and cheeks in pink into the base of each bowl. Pipe 6 brown dots for eyes on baking pan. Bake at 160°C for $1^{1}/_{2}$ minutes.

5. Pour pandan batter equally into glass bowls until about half full leaving some for the eyes and legs. Pour remaining pandan batter into baking pan for sheet cake. Gently tap bowls and pan on counter top to release any air bubbles.

6. Place bowls on lowest rack of oven and steam bake at 150°C for 35–40 minutes or until a skewer inserted into centre of cakes comes out clean. Bake sheet cake at 160°C for 10 minutes.

7. Invert bowls on a wire rack to cool completely before unmoulding. Invert sheet cake on baking paper and let cool.

8. Peel baking paper from sheet cake and place on a cutting mat. Use a round cutter slightly larger than the size of brown eyes to cut 8 eye sockets from sheet cake. Use a flower cutter to cut out 8 shapes, then trim to form feet. Assemble parts using marshmallow cream.

Pumpkin Jack O'Lantern Cupcakes

Makes eight 7-cm cupcakes

 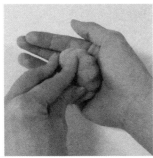  

Egg yolk batter

2 egg yolks

10 g castor sugar

27 g vegetable/corn oil

1 tsp water

40 g pumpkin purée (made by steaming, then mashing pumpkin through a sieve)

$1/4$ tsp vanilla extract

40 g cake flour, sifted

$1/8$ tsp ground cinnamon, sifted

$1/4$ tsp baking powder, sifted

A pinch of salt

$1/2$ tsp charcoal powder, sifted

Orange gel food colouring

Meringue

3 egg whites

$1/5$ tsp cream of tartar

30 g castor sugar

Finishing

Cinnamon sticks or chocolate twirls or shavings, cut into short lengths

Marshmallow cream (page 24)

1. Preheat oven to 160°C. Prepare 8 metal jelly moulds, each about 7 cm in diameter. Line a 15-cm square baking pan with baking paper.

2. Prepare egg yolk batter (page 20). Spoon 3 tsp batter into a small bowl and add $1/2$ tsp charcoal powder. Mix well. Add a few drops orange colouring to remaining batter.

3. Prepare meringue (page 20). Fold 6 Tbsp meringue into black batter one-third at a time. Pour black batter into baking pan and tap pan on counter top to release any air bubbles. Fold remaining meringue into orange batter one-third at a time. Spoon orange batter into metal jelly moulds until they are three-quarters full.

4. Bake black sheet cake at 160°C for 9–10 minutes, then invert cake onto a sheet of baking paper and let cool.

5. Bake orange cupcakes at 160°C for 10 minutes, then 140°C for 15–20 minutes, or until a skewer inserted into centre of cakes comes out clean. Place cupcakes on a wire rack to cool completely before unmoulding.

6. Place a cupcake in your palm and with the other hand, press to tuck in base of cupcakes so cakes appear more spherical.

7. Peel baking paper from black sheet cake and place on a cutting mat. Use a nori sheet cutter or cookie cutter to cut out eyes and mouths from sheet cake. Create any expression you want. Assemble features using marshmallow cream.

8. Insert a cinnamon stick, chocolate twirl or shavings at the top of each cupcake for the stem.

Vanilla-Lemon Rocking Horse Cupcakes

Makes 10–12 cupcakes

Vanilla-lemon chiffon

Egg yolk batter

2 egg yolks

10 g castor sugar

28 g vegetable/corn oil

26 g fresh milk

1 tsp fresh lemon juice

Finely grated zest of ½ lemon

1 tsp vanilla extract

40 g cake flour, sifted

A pinch of salt

Meringue

3 egg whites

⅛ tsp cream of tartar

30 g castor sugar

Coloured sheet cakes

Egg yolk batter

1 egg yolk

10 g castor sugar

40 g vegetable/corn oil

40 g water

½ tsp vanilla extract

60 g cake flour, sifted

A pinch of salt

A pinch of charcoal powder, sifted

Pink, purple, white
   gel food colouring

Meringue

4 egg whites

¼ tsp cream of tartar

40 g castor sugar

1. Preheat oven to 160°C. Prepare 10–12 waxed cupcake cups.

2. Prepare egg yolk batter (page 20) and meringue (page 20) for vanilla-lemon chiffon. Gently fold meringue into egg yolk batter one-third at a time. Fill cupcake cases until batter is about 1 cm away from rim.

3. Bake at 160°C for 8 minutes, then 140°C for 9–15 minutes, or until a skewer inserted into centre of cakes comes out clean. Let cool.

4. Prepare coloured sheet cakes. Line a 25-cm x 30-cm baking pan and two 15-cm square baking pans with baking paper.

5. Prepare egg yolk batter (page 20) for coloured sheet cakes. Spoon ½ tsp batter into a small bowl and add charcoal powder. Spoon 3 tsp batter into another bowl and colour it dark pink. Spoon 3 tsp batter into a third bowl and colour it purple. Divide rest of batter into 2 equal portions. Colour one portion light pink and leave the other portion uncoloured or add a few drops of white colouring if desired.

6. Prepare meringue (page 20) for coloured sheet cakes. Add 1 Tbsp meringue to black batter, 6 Tbsp meringue to dark pink batter and 6 Tbsp meringue to purple batter. Divide remaining meringue into 2 portions and fold into light pink and white batters a third at a time.

7. Pour coloured batters onto individual baking pans. Gently tap pans on counter top to release any air bubbles. Bake at 160°C for 10 minutes, then invert sheet cakes on baking paper to cool.

8. Peel baking paper from sheet cakes and place on a cutting mat. Use a 6-cm round cutter to cut light pink and white circles from sheet cakes. Adhere to cupcakes using marshmallow cream.

9. Use a rocking horse cookie cutter to cut out light pink and white horses, then use corresponding parts of cutter to cut out mane, tail and base from dark pink and purple sheet cakes.

10. Use a small fruit knife to cut out horse body from light pink and white horses. Use the knife to cut out 6 purple saddles. Use a small straw to cut out 6 eyes from black sheet cake. Assemble parts using marshmallow cream. Brush cupcakes with syrup.

Orange Sunflower Cupcakes

Makes 16 cupcakes

Recipe on pages 60 and 61

Orange chiffon

Egg yolk batter

3 egg yolks

15 g castor sugar

42 g vegetable/corn oil

42 g orange juice

$1/3$ tsp orange emulco (optional)

7 g finely grated orange zest

60 g cake flour, sifted

$1/4$ tsp baking powder, sifted

$1/8$ tsp salt

Meringue

4 egg whites

$1/5$ tsp cream of tartar

40 g castor sugar

Yellow orange chiffon

Egg yolk batter

4 egg yolks

20 g castor sugar

56 g vegetable/corn oil

56 g orange juice

1 g finely grated orange zest

1 tsp orange emulco

80 g cake flour, sifted

$1/8$ tsp salt

Yellow gel food colouring

Meringue

5 egg whites

$1/4$ tsp cream of tartar

50 g castor sugar

1. Preheat oven to 160°C. Prepare 16 waxed cupcake cups.

2. Prepare egg yolk batter (page 20) and meringue (page 20) for orange chiffon.

3. Gently fold meringue into egg yolk batter one-third at a time. Fill cupcake cases until batter is about 1 cm away from rim.

4. Bake at 160°C for 8 minutes, then 140°C for 9–15 minutes or until a skewer inserted into centre of cakes comes out clean. Let cool.

5. Prepare yellow orange chiffon. Line two 25-cm x 30-cm and two 15-cm square baking pans with baking paper.

6. Prepare egg yolk batter (page 20) for yellow orange chiffon. Divide batter into 2 equal portions.

7. Divide meringue ingredients for yellow orange chiffon into 2 equal portions. Prepare meringue for one portion (page 20).

8. Gently fold meringue into one portion of egg yolk batter one-third at a time. Pour three-quarters of the batter into a 25-cm x 30-cm pan and the remaining batter in a 15-cm square pan. Gently tap pans on counter top to release any air bubbles.

9. Bake at 160°C for 9–10 minutes. Invert cakes onto a sheet of baking paper and set aside to cool.

10. Repeat for other portion of egg yolk batter and meringue.

Chocolate chiffon

Egg yolk batter

1 egg yolk

5 g castor sugar

15 g vegetable/corn oil

15 g fresh milk

1/2 tsp vanilla extract

18 g cake flour, sifted

1 tsp cocoa powder, sifted

1/4 tsp charcoal powder, sifted

A pinch of salt

Meringue

1 1/2 egg whites

A pinch of cream of tartar

15 g castor sugar

Finishing

Marshmallow cream (page 24)

Golden yellow gel food colouring

Syrup (page 24)

Note You may bake the sheet cakes in advance, double-wrap them with plastic wrap, place in big sealable bags and freeze until it is time for assembly.

---

11. Prepare egg yolk batter (page 20) and meringue (page 20) for chocolate chiffon.

12. Gently fold meringue into egg yolk batter one-third at a time. Pour batter into a 25-cm x 30-cm pan. Gently tap pan on counter top to release any air bubbles.

13. Bake at 160°C for 9–10 minutes. Invert sheet cake onto a sheet of baking paper and let cool.

14. Peel baking paper from sheet cake and place on a cutting mat. Use a 7-cm sunflower/daisy cutter to cut out 32 flower shapes from yellow sheet cakes. Use a 3.5-cm round cutter to cut out 16 circles from chocolate sheet cake. Keep cut outs in an airtight container or cover with plastic wrap to prevent drying.

15. Level off the top of cupcakes if they have a noticeable dome, so it is level with the cupcake cup.

16. Apply some marshmallow cream to the top of each cupcake and place a flower cut out over it. Repeat to apply some marshmallow cream on flower cut out and top with another flower cut out, then apply some marshmallow cream on second flower cut out and top with a circle for centre of flower.

17. To make the sunflowers more realistic, use a fruit knife to make a small incision from the centre of flower until 2–3 mm from the tip of each petal.

18. Mix a little golden yellow food colouring with a bit of syrup and paint each petal along the incision. Gently press brush into each incision to create a deeper indent.

19. Brush surface of flowers with syrup to keep cakes moist.

Let's Celebrate!

Rainbow Layer Cake

Makes one 18-cm cake

Egg yolk batter

5 egg yolks

33 g castor sugar

65 g vegetable/corn oil

70 g water

1¹/₂ tsp vanilla extract

100 g cake flour, sifted

A pinch of salt

Pink, orange, yellow, green, blue
and purple gel food colouring

Meringue

7 egg whites

¹/₄ tsp cream of tartar

75 g castor sugar

1. Preheat oven to 160°C. Prepare an 18-cm round chiffon tube pan.

2. Prepare egg yolk batter (page 20). Spoon batter equally into 6 small bowls (approximately 10 tsp batter per bowl). Add a different food colouring to each bowl and mix well.

3. Prepare meringue (page 20). Divide meringue into 6 equal portions and add a portion to each coloured batter. Gently fold meringue into each egg yolk batter one-third at a time.

4. Spoon pink batter into chiffon pan. Gently level batter. Repeat with orange, yellow, green, blue and purple batters, taking care not to disturb previous layer. Gently tap pan on counter top to release any air bubbles.

5. Bake at 160°C for 15 minutes, then 140°C for 31 minutes, or until a skewer inserted into the centre of cake comes out clean.

6. Invert pan on a wire rack to cool completely before unmoulding.

Twinkle Stars Ombre Blue Cake

Makes one 23-cm cake

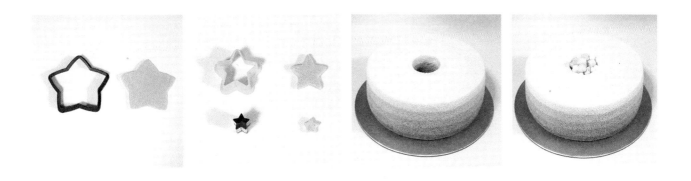

Ombre vanilla chiffon

Egg yolk batter

6 egg yolks

53 g castor sugar

106 g vegetable/corn oil

100 g water

1 Tbsp vanilla extract

160 g cake flour, sifted

A pinch of salt

Blue and purple gel food colouring

Charcoal powder

Meringue

11 egg whites

$^1/_2$ tsp cream of tartar

120 g castor sugar

Yellow sheet cake

Egg Yolk Batter

1 egg yolk

9 g castor sugar

15 g vegetable/corn oil

16 g water

$^1/_2$ tsp vanilla extract

26 g cake flour, sifted

A pinch of salt

Yellow gel food colouring

Meringue

2 egg whites

$^1/_4$ tsp cream of tartar

15 g castor sugar

Finishing

Marshmallow cream (page 24)

1. Preheat oven to 160°C. Prepare a 23-cm round chiffon tube pan.

2. Prepare egg yolk batter (page 20) for ombre vanilla chiffon. Divide batter equally into 5 bowls. Set one bowl aside. To other 4 bowls, add a little blue colouring, increasing the amount for each bowl to get a darker blue. To the darkest batter, add a little purple colouring and charcoal powder to get a navy blue shade.

3. Prepare meringue (page 20) for ombre vanilla chiffon. Divide meringue into 5 equal portions. Gently fold meringue into each egg yolk batter one-third at a time.

4. Spoon plain batter into chiffon pan. Gently level batter. Repeat with light blue batter, followed by darker blue and ending with navy blue batter, taking care not to disrupt previous layer. Gently tap pan on counter top thrice to release any air bubbles.

5. Bake at 160°C for 15 minutes, then 150°C for 10 minutes, 140°C for 20 minutes and 130°C for 15 minutes, or until a skewer inserted into the centre of cake comes out clean.

6. Invert pan on a wire rack to cool completely before unmoulding.

7. Preheat oven to 160°C. Line a 20-cm square baking pan with baking paper.

8. Prepare egg yolk batter (page 20) and meringue (page 20) for yellow sheet cake. Gently fold meringue into egg yolk batter one-third at a time. Pour batter into prepared pan. Gently tap pan on counter top to release any air bubbles.

9. Bake at 160°C for 9–10 minutes. Invert sheet cake onto a sheet of baking paper and let cool.

10. Peel baking paper from sheet cake and place on a cutting mat. Use a large star cutter to cut out a large yellow star. Use smaller star cutters to cut out smaller stars.

11. Fill centre of cake with marshmallows or sweets for a hidden surprise. Place large star over to conceal surprise. Adhere stars to cake using marshmallow cream.

Neapolitan Polka-dotted Cake

Makes one 18-cm cake

Chocolate chiffon

Egg yolk batter

2 egg yolks

17 g castor sugar

30 g vegetable/corn oil

33 g water

1 tsp vanilla extract

40 g cake flour, sifted

13 g cocoa powder

1/4 tsp baking powder

A pinch of salt

Meringue

3 egg whites

1/4 tsp cream of tartar

30 g castor sugar

Strawberry chiffon

Egg Yolk Batter

1 egg yolk

10 g castor sugar

20 g vegetable/corn oil

22 g strawberry purée

30 g cake flour, sifted

A pinch of salt

1/4 tsp strawberry paste

Meringue

2 egg whites

1/4 tsp cream of tartar

23 g castor sugar

Vanilla chiffon

Egg Yolk Batter

1 egg yolk

10 g castor sugar

20 g vegetable/corn oil

18 g water

1 tsp vanilla extract

30 g cake flour, sifted

A pinch of salt

Meringue

2 egg whites

1/4 tsp cream of tartar

23 g castor sugar

Finishing

Marshmallow cream (page 24)

1. Preheat oven to 160°C. Prepare an 18-cm round chiffon tube pan, and line a 15-cm square baking pan and a 23-cm square baking pan with baking paper.

2. Prepare egg yolk batter (page 20) and meringue (page 20) for chocolate chiffon and strawberry chiffon. Gently fold meringue into each egg yolk batter one-third at a time.

3. Pour chocolate chiffon batter into base of tube pan until about two-thirds full. Gently spoon strawberry chiffon batter over chocolate layer, being careful not to disturb chocolate layer, until batter is about 2 cm from rim of pan. Set remaining batter aside.

4. Gently tap pan on counter top to release any air bubbles. Bake at 160°C for 15 minutes, then 140°C for 30 minutes, or until a skewer inserted into centre of cake comes out clean.

5. Invert pan on a wire rack to cool completely before unmoulding.

6. Preheat oven to 160°C.

7. Pour remaining strawberry chiffon batter into prepared 15-cm baking pan. Gently tap pan on counter top to release any air bubbles. Bake at 160°C for 14 minutes. Invert cake onto a sheet of baking paper and let cool.

8. Prepare egg yolk batter (page 20) and meringue (page 20) for vanilla chiffon. Gently fold meringue into egg yolk batter one-third at a time.

9. Pour batter into prepared 23-cm baking pan. Gently tap pan on counter top to release any air bubbles. Bake at 160°C for 14 minutes. Invert sheet cakes on a sheet of baking paper and let cool.

10. Peel baking paper from sheet cakes. Place on cutting mats. Use a bow cutter to cut out a bow from strawberry chiffon and round cutters to cut circles from vanilla chiffon. Adhere to cake using marshmallow cream.

Snowflake Cake

Makes one 18-cm cake

Egg yolk batter

2 egg yolks

33 g castor sugar

65 g vegetable/corn oil

70 g water

1¹/₂ tsp vanilla extract

100 g cake flour, sifted

A pinch of salt

1¹/₂ tsp blue pea flower extract
   (page 25)

Blue gel food colouring

Meringue

7 egg whites

¹/₄ tsp cream of tartar

75 g castor sugar

Finishing

Marshmallow cream (page 24)

1. Preheat oven to 160°C. Prepare an 18-cm chiffon tube pan and line two 23-cm square baking pans with baking paper.

2. Prepare egg yolk batter (page 20). Divide batter equally into 2 bowls. Add blue pea flower extract and a little blue colouring to one portion. Leave the other portion plain.

3. Prepare meringue (page 20). Divide meringue into 2 portions and gently fold into each batter one-third at a time.

4. Pour some plain batter into chiffon tube pan to create a base layer about 2.5-cm thick. With remaining plain batter, create mounds by dropping spoonfuls of batter at intervals close to sides of pan. Smoothen edge of mounds using a chopstick.

5. Spoon blue batter to fill spaces between mounds, then top with remaining blue batter until batter is about 2 cm from rim of pan. Gently tap pan on counter top to release any air bubbles.

6. Bake at 160°C for 15 minutes, then 140°C for 31 minutes, or until a skewer inserted into centre of cake comes out clean.

7. Invert pan on a wire rack to cool completely before unmoulding.

8. Preheat oven to 160°C.

9. Pour remaining blue and white batters separately into two 23-cm square baking pans. Gently tap pans on counter top to release any air bubbles. Bake at 160°C for 14 minutes. Invert cake onto a sheet of baking paper and let cool.

10. Peel baking paper from blue and white sheet cakes and place on a cutting mat. Use a large snowflake cutter to cut a large snowflake from the white sheet cake and a medium snowflake cutter to cut a medium snowflake from blue cake. Use smaller snowflake cutters to cut out smaller snowflakes.

11. Fill centre of cake with marshmallows or sweets for a hidden surprise. Place large snowflake over to conceal surprise. Adhere snowflakes to cake using marshmallow cream.

Six-flavour Rainbow Hearts Cake

Makes one 18-cm cake

Red	1 tsp strawberry purée + $^1/_5$ tsp strawberry paste
Orange	1 tsp orange juice + zest from $^1/_3$ orange + $^1/_5$ tsp orange paste
Yellow	1 tsp lemon juice + zest from $^1/_3$ lemon + $^1/_5$ tsp lemon paste
Green	1 tsp pandan juice (page 25) + $^1/_5$ tsp pandan paste
Blue	1 tsp blue pea flower extract (page 25) + $^1/_5$ tsp vanilla extract + a little blue gel food colouring
Purple	$^1/_2$ tsp blueberry powder + $^2/_5$ tsp blueberry extract + $^4/_5$ tsp water

Sheet cake

Egg yolk batter

2 egg yolks

13 g castor sugar

23 g vegetable/corn oil

30 g water

40 g cake flour, sifted

A pinch of salt

Meringue

3 egg whites

$^1/_5$ tsp cream of tartar

30 g castor sugar

6-flavour chiffon

Egg yolk batter

4 egg yolks

27 g castor sugar

47 g vegetable/corn oil

53 g water

80 g cake flour, sifted

Meringue

6 egg whites

$^1/_4$ tsp cream of tartar

60 g castor sugar

1. Preheat oven to 160°C. Line a 25-cm square baking pan with baking paper.

2. Prepare egg yolk batter (page 20) and meringue (page 20) for sheet cake. Gently fold meringue into egg yolk batter one-third at a time.

3. Pour batter into prepared pan. Gently tap pan on counter top to release any air bubbles. Bake at 160°C for 14 minutes.

4. Invert sheet cake onto a sheet of baking paper and let cool. Cut sheet cake into 6 small squares corresponding to width of chiffon pan. Use a heart-shape cutter to cut out 6 hearts from remaining sheet cake.

5. Prepare egg yolk batter (page 20) for 6-flavour chiffon. Spoon batter equally into 6 small bowls. Add colouring and flavouring for each colour, as suggested in table, to each bowl. Mix well.

6. Prepare meringue (page 20). Divide meringue into 6 equal parts and gently fold into each batter in 2 additions.

7. Arrange heart cut outs on base of chiffon pan, and cake squares vertically in pan to create 6 segments.

8. Spoon a different colour batter into each segment, doing this gently but quickly to avoid deflating batter. Gently tap pan on counter top to release any air bubbles.

9. Bake at 160°C for 15 minutes, then 150°C for 15 minutes and 140°C for 15 minutes, or until a skewer inserted into the centre of cake comes out clean.

10. Invert pan on a wire rack to cool completely before unmoulding.

Rainbow Tier Cake

Makes one 10-cm and one 15-cm cake

Recipe on pages 76 and 77

Pink strawberry chiffon

Egg yolk batter

1 egg yolk

7 g castor sugar

13 g vegetable/corn oil

16 g strawberry purée

20 g cake flour, sifted

A pinch of salt

$1/4$ tsp strawberry paste

Meringue

2 egg whites

$1/4$ tsp cream of tartar

10 g castor sugar

Green pandan chiffon

Egg yolk batter

2 egg yolks

13 g castor sugar

26 g vegetable/corn oil

16 g coconut milk

$1^1/2$ tsp pandan juice (page 25)

$1/5$ tsp vanilla extract

$1/2$ tsp pandan paste

40 g cake flour, sifted

A pinch of salt

Meringue

3 egg whites

$1/4$ tsp cream of tartar

30 g castor sugar

1. Preheat oven to 160°C. Prepare a 10-cm chiffon tube pan.

2. Prepare egg yolk batter (page 20) and meringue (page 20) for pink strawberry chiffon. Gently fold meringue into egg yolk batter one-third at a time.

3. Pour batter into 10-cm chiffon pan. Gently tap pan on counter top to release any air bubbles. Bake at 160°C for 10 minutes, then 150°C for 10 minutes, or until a skewer inserted into the centre of cake comes out clean.

4. Invert pan on a wire rack to cool completely before unmoulding.

5. Preheat oven to 160°C. Prepare a 15-cm chiffon tube pan.

6. Prepare egg yolk batter (page 20) and meringue (page 20) for green pandan chiffon. Gently fold meringue into egg yolk batter one-third at a time.

7. Pour batter into 15-cm chiffon pan and bake at 160°C for 15 minutes, then 140°C for 25–30 minutes.

8. Invert pan on a wire rack to cool completely before unmoulding.

Coloured sheet cake

Egg yolk batter

2 egg yolks

14 g castor sugar

26 g vegetable/corn oil

24 g water

1 tsp vanilla extract

40 g cake flour, sifted

A pinch of salt

Yellow, blue and purple
  gel food colouring

Meringue

3 egg whites

$1/4$ tsp cream of tartar

30 g castor sugar

Finishing

Marshmallow cream (page 24)

Icing flowers, if desired

> *Note* When attempting to make multi-tier chiffon cakes like this one, the top tier has to be small and light to avoid it pressing down on the bottom tier.
>
> For a larger top tier, you may need to use dowel rods to support the tiers.

---

9. Preheat oven to 160°C and line a 25-cm square baking pan with baking paper.

10. Prepare egg yolk batter (page 20) for coloured sheet cake. Divide batter into 2 equal portions. Add a little yellow colouring to one portion and mix well. Add a little blue and purple colouring to the other and mix well.

11. Prepare meringue (page 20) for coloured sheet cake. Divide meringue into 2 equal portions and gently fold into each batter one-third at a time.

12. Pour yellow and blue/purple batters side by side into prepared 25-cm pan. Gently tap pan on counter top to release any air bubbles.

13. Bake at 160°C for 14 minutes. Invert sheet cake onto a sheet of baking paper and let cool.

14. Brush base of pink 10-cm cake with marshmallow cream and arrange on top of 15-cm green cake.

15. Peel baking paper from yellow and blue/purple sheet cake and place on a cutting mat. Cut a thin strip from each colour. Adhere strips to cake using marshmallow cream.

16. Use a butterfly cutter to cut out butterflies from leftover sheet cake. Adhere to cake using marshmallow cream.

17. Decorate cake with icing flowers if desired.

Busy Road Cake

Makes one 23-cm cake

Recipe on pages 80 and 81

Blue and green chiffon

Egg yolk batter

8 egg yolks

53 g castor sugar

105 g vegetable/corn oil

101 g water

2 1/2 tsp vanilla extract

160 g cake flour, sifted

A pinch of salt

2 tsp blue pea flower extract
(page 25)

Blue gel food colouring

1 tsp pandan paste

17 g coconut cream powder

Meringue

11 egg whites

1/2 tsp cream of tartar

120 g castor sugar

1. Preheat oven to 160°C. Prepare a 23-cm chiffon tube pan.

2. Prepare egg yolk batter (page 20) for blue and green chiffon. Divide batter into 2 equal portions. Add blue pea flower extract and a little blue colouring to one portion and mix well. Add pandan paste and coconut cream powder to other portion and mix well.

3. Prepare meringue (page 20) for blue and green chiffon. Divide meringue into 2 equal portions and gently fold into each batter one-third at a time.

4. Pour some blue batter into chiffon tube pan to create a base layer about 3-cm thick. With remaining blue batter, create mounds by dropping spoonfuls of batter at intervals, close to sides of pan. Smoothen edge of mounds using a chopstick.

5. Spoon green batter to fill spaces between mounds, then top with remaining green batter until batter is about 2 cm from rim of pan. Gently tap pan on counter top to release any air bubbles.

6. Bake at 160°C for 15 minutes, 150°C for 10 minutes, 140°C for 20 minutes and 130°C for 15 minutes, or until a skewer inserted into centre of cake comes out clean.

7. Invert pan on a wire rack to cool completely before unmoulding.

Coloured sheet cakes

Egg yolk batter

3 egg yolks

20 g castor sugar

39 g vegetable/corn oil

41 g water

1 tsp vanilla extract

60 g cake flour, sifted

Red, orange, green and black
  gel food colouring

Meringue

4 egg whites

1/4 tsp cream of tartar

45 g castor sugar

Finishing

Marshmallow cream (page 24)

8. Preheat oven to 160°C. Line two 20-cm square baking pans and one 12-cm square baking pan with baking paper.

9. Prepare egg yolk batter (page 20) for coloured sheet cakes. Divide batter into 5 equal portions. Add a little food colouring to 4 portions to colour them each a different colour. Mix well. Leave the last portion plain.

10. Prepare meringue (page 20) for coloured sheet cakes. Divide meringue into 5 equal portions and gently fold into each batter one-third at a time.

11. Pour red and orange batters side by side into prepared 20-cm baking pan. Repeat for black and green batters. Pour plain batter into prepared 12-cm baking pan. Gently tap pans on counter top to release any air bubbles.

12. Bake at 160°C for 14 minutes. Invert each sheet cake onto a sheet of baking paper and let cool.

13. Peel baking paper from black and green sheet cake and place on a cutting mat. Use a small round cutter or large straw to cut 5 circles from black cake for wheels — 3 for truck and 2 for car. Use a medium round cutter to cut a circle from green cake, then cut circle into quarters for windows.

14. Peel baking paper from red and orange sheet cake and place on a cutting mat. Use a truck cutter to cut truck shape from orange cake. Cut off truck cabin with a knife and use a round cutter to cut off wheels. Use truck cutter to cut same shape from red cake and repeat to cut off cabin portion. Replace orange cabin with red cabin and orange wheels with black wheels. Place green window on cabin and adhere with marshmallow cream.

15. Use a car cutter to cut out car shape from red cake and use a round cutter to cut off wheels. Replace red wheels with black wheels. Place green windows on car and adhere with marshmallow cream. Cut one of the discarded orange circles in half for headlight of car.

16. To make traffic lights, use a round cutter to cut circles from red, orange and green sheet cakes. Use a knife to cut a rectangle for traffic light and a narrow strip for pole from black sheet cake.

17. Peel baking paper from plain sheet cake and place on a cutting mat. Use a cloud cutter to cut out cloud shapes.

18. Assemble parts on cake using marshmallow cream.

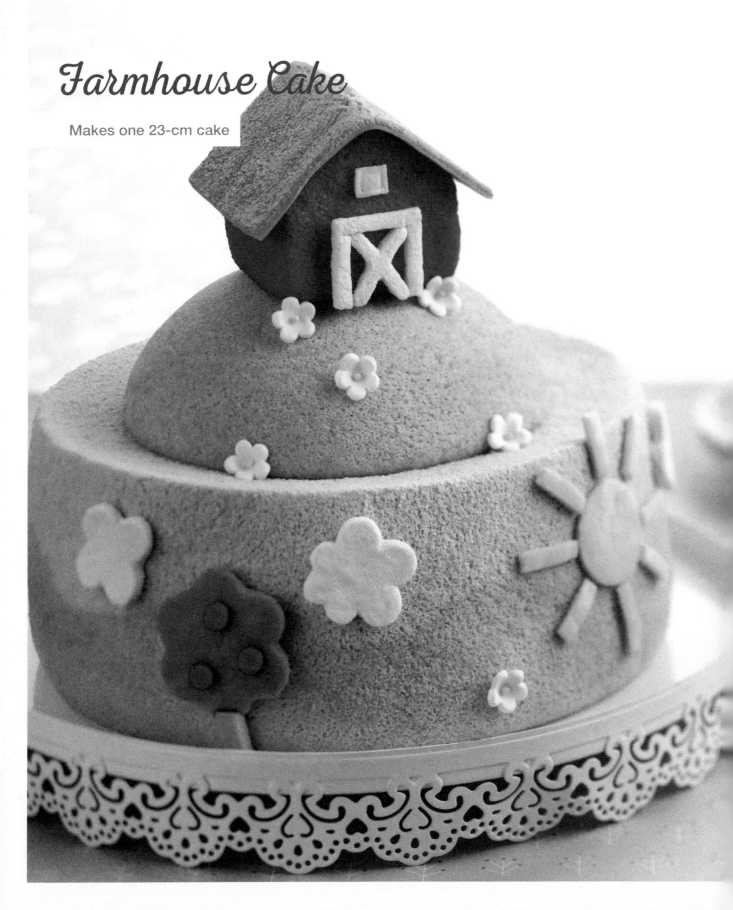

Farmhouse Cake

Makes one 23-cm cake

Recipe on pages 84 and 85

Blue and green chiffon

Egg yolk batter

10 egg yolks

66 g castor sugar

131 g vegetable/corn oil

126 g water

200 g cake flour, sifted

1 Tbsp vanilla extract

Blue pea flower extract (page 25)

Blue gel food colouring

1½ tsp pandan paste

21 g coconut cream powder

A pinch of salt

Meringue chiffon pan cake

14 egg whites

½ tsp cream of tartar

150 g castor sugar

Meringue for mound cake

3 egg whites

¼ tsp cream of tartar

30 g castor sugar

1. Preheat oven to 160°C. Prepare a 23-cm chiffon tube pan.

2. Prepare egg yolk batter (page 20) for blue and green chiffon. Spoon 40 tsp (13⅓ Tbsp) batter into another bowl and add a little blue pea flower extract and blue colouring to make a sky blue batter. Mix well. Add pandan paste, coconut cream powder and salt to remaining batter and mix well.

3. Spoon 20 tsp (6⅔ Tbsp) pandan batter into another bowl for mound cake.

4. Prepare meringue (page 20) for chiffon pan cake. Spoon 80 Tbsp (5 cups) meringue into another bowl and gently fold into blue batter one-third at a time. Fold remaining meringue into pandan batter one-third at a time.

5. Pour some blue batter into chiffon tube pan to create a base layer about 2-cm thick. With remaining blue batter, create mounds by dropping spoonfuls of batter at intervals, close to sides of pan. Smoothen edge of mounds using a chopstick.

6. Spoon green batter to fill spaces between mounds, then top with remaining green batter until batter is about 2 cm from rim of pan. Gently tap pan on counter top to release any air bubbles.

7. Bake at 160°C for 15 minutes, 150°C for 10 minutes, 140°C for 20 minutes and 130°C for 15 minutes, or until a skewer inserted into centre of cake comes out clean.

8. Invert pan on a wire rack to cool completely before unmoulding.

9. Preheat oven to 160°C. Prepare a 15-cm round glass bowl and line a 15-cm square baking pan with baking paper.

10. Prepare meringue (page 20) for mound cake and gently fold into reserved pandan batter one-third at a time.

11. Pour some batter into glass bowl until three-quarters full. Bake at 160°C for 15 minutes, then 140°C for 20 minutes. Invert bowl on a wire rack and let cool.

12. Preheat oven to 160°C.

13. Pour remaining pandan batter into 15-cm pan and bake at 160°C for 14 minutes. Invert sheet cake onto a sheet of baking paper and let cool.

Coloured sheet cakes

Egg yolk batter

1 egg yolk

13 g castor sugar

23 g vegetable/corn oil

25 g water

1 tsp vanilla extract

40 g cake flour, sifted

A pinch of salt

1/4 tsp strawberry paste

1/4 tsp red yeast powder

1/2 tsp cocoa powder

Yellow gel food colouring

Meringue

3 egg whites

1/4 tsp cream of tartar

30 g castor sugar

Finishing

Marshmallow cream (page 24)

Icing flowers, if desired

14. Preheat oven to 160°C. Prepare a gingerbread house silicone mould and line a 25-cm square baking pan and an 18-cm square baking pan with baking paper.

15. Prepare egg yolk batter (page 20) for coloured sheet cakes. Divide batter into 4 equal portions. Add strawberry paste and red yeast powder to one bowl to make a red batter, cocoa powder to another bowl for brown batter, and a little yellow colouring to a third bowl for yellow batter. Leave the last portion plain.

16. Prepare meringue (page 20) for coloured sheet cakes. Divide meringue into 4 equal portions and gently fold into each batter one-third at a time.

17. Pour red batter into gingerbread house mould and bake at 160°C for 15 minutes, then at 140°C for 15 minutes, or until a skewer inserted into centre of cake comes out clean.

18. Invert mould on a wire rack to cool completely before unmoulding.

19. Preheat oven to 160°C.

20. Pour brown and yellow batters side by side into prepared 25-cm pan and white and remaining red batters into 18-cm pan. Gently tap pans on counter top to release any air bubbles. Bake at 160°C for 14 minutes.

21. Invert each sheet cake onto a sheet of baking paper and let cool.

22. Peel baking paper from brown and yellow sheet cake and place on a cutting mat. Use a round cutter to cut a circle from yellow cake for the sun and 8 strips for sun rays.

23. Peel baking paper from white and red sheet cake and place on a cutting mat. Use a flower cutter to cut a tree shape from green cake. Use a knife to cut a strip from brown cake for tree trunk. Use a small round cutter to cut 3 circles from red cake for fruit.

24. Use a cloud cutter to cut out clouds from white cake.

25. Use a knife to cut a window and door from white cake. Cut a big brown rectangle from brown cake for roof. Assemble parts using marshmallow cream.

26. Fill centre of cake with marshmallows or sweets for a hidden surprise. Place green mound cake over to conceal surprise.

27. Place house on green mound cake and adhere using marshmallow cream. Decorate with icing flowers if desired.

Flowers in Bloom Cake

Makes one 15-cm cake

Recipe on pages 88 and 89

Low-sugar Earl Grey Honey Chiffon

Earl Grey-infused milk

30 g milk

1 Tbsp (20 g) honey

1–2 Earl Grey tea bags

1/2 tsp dried lavender flowers

Egg yolk batter

2 egg yolks

2 g castor sugar (or 25 g castor sugar for regular chiffon)

27 g vegetable/corn oil

27 g Earl Grey-infused milk

1 tsp vanilla extract

40 g cake flour, sifted

A pinch of salt

2 g instant Earl Grey powder, sifted

Meringue

3 egg whites

1/5 tsp cream of tartar

28 g castor sugar

1. Prepare Earl Grey-infused milk for Earl Grey honey chiffon cake. Heat milk over low heat. Add honey and stir until honey is dissolved. Steep tea bags and dried lavender flowers in hot milk for 5–10 minutes. Squeeze tea bags to extract as much tea as possible and strain lavender flowers. Measure out 27 g for use in egg yolk batter.

2. Preheat oven to 160°C. Prepare a 15-cm chiffon tube pan.

3. Prepare egg yolk batter (page 20) with Earl Grey-infused milk for Earl Grey honey chiffon.

4. Prepare meringue (page 20) for Earl Grey honey chiffon.

5. Gently fold meringue into egg yolk batter one-third at a time. Pour batter into chiffon pan and tap pan on counter top to release any air bubbles.

6. Bake at 160°C for 15 minutes, 150°C for 10 minutes, 140°C for 15–20 minutes, or until a skewer inserted into centre of cake comes out clean.

7. Invert pan on a wire rack to cool completely before unmoulding.

Coloured sheet cakes

Egg yolk batter

1 egg yolk

10 g castor sugar

40 g vegetable/corn oil

40 g water

¹/₄ tsp vanilla extract

60 g cake flour, sifted

A pinch of salt

White, pink, red and green
  gel food colouring

Meringue

4 egg whites

¹/₄ tsp cream of tartar

40 g castor sugar

Finishing

Marshmallow cream (page 24)

Syrup (page 24)

8. Preheat oven to 160°C. Line two 25-cm x 30-cm baking pans with baking paper.

9. Prepare egg yolk batter (page 20) for coloured sheet cakes. Divide batter into 4 equal portions. Add a different food colouring to each portion and mix well.

10. Prepare meringue (page 20) for coloured sheet cakes. Divide meringue into 4 equal portions and gently fold into each batter one-third at a time.

11. Pour white and pink batters side by side into a prepared baking tray. Repeat with red and green batters. Gently tap pans on counter top to release any air bubbles. Bake at 160°C for 10 minutes.

12. Invert each sheet cake onto a sheet of baking paper and let cool.

13. Peel baking paper from sheet cakes and place each sheet cake on a cutting mat.

14. To make roses, use a round cutter to cut out 3 circles per rose from white, pink and red sheet cakes. Cut circles in half. Overlap the 6 semi-circles slightly and spoon a thin line of marshmallow cream across the row of semi-circles. Roll semi circles up tightly to create a rose.

15. To make daisies, use daisy cutters to cut out shapes from pink and red sheet cakes. Use a round cutter to cut circles from white sheet cake for centre of daisies. Stick circles onto daisy base with marshmallow cream.

16. Use a large round cutter to cut a circle from green layer cake to cover hole in centre of chiffon cake. Use a leaf cutter to cut leaves from remaining green sheet cake.

17. Assemble flowers and leaves on top of Earl Grey honey chiffon with marshmallow cream.

18. Brush some syrup on flowers and leaves to keep them moist.

It's All
in the Cake!

Orange Wheel Cake

Makes one 18-cm cake

Orange chiffon

Egg yolk batter

3 egg yolks

20 g castor sugar

39 g vegetable/corn oil

41 g orange juice

1 orange, finely grated for zest

60 g cake flour, sifted

A pinch of salt

$1/4$ tsp charcoal powder

A few drops orange emulco

Meringue for pattern

1 egg white

$1/5$ tsp cream of tartar

11 g castor sugar

Meringue for chiffon cake

4 egg whites

$1/4$ tsp cream of tartar

45 g castor sugar

1. Preheat oven to 160°C. Prepare an 18-cm chiffon tube pan.

2. Prepare egg yolk batter (page 20). Spoon 3 tsp batter into a small bowl for pattern batter. Add charcoal powder and mix well. Spoon 5 tsp batter into another bowl and set aside as plain batter. Add orange emulco to remaining batter and mix well.

3. Prepare meringue (page 20) for pattern. Gently fold meringue into charcoal batter one-third at a time.

4. Spoon batter for pattern into a piping bag and cut a 3-mm hole at the tip. Pipe batter to create rings and lines for wheel. Ensure to pipe thick lines so pattern will form nicely and not stick to base of chiffon pan when cake is unmoulded. Bake at 160°C for $1^1/2$ minutes. Set pan aside.

5. Prepare meringue (page 20) for chiffon cake. Gently fold 10 Tbsp meringue into 5 tsp plain batter one-third at a time. Gently fold remaining meringue into orange emulco batter one-third at a time.

6. Using a teaspoon, spoon plain batter into inner ring of wheel. Repeat to spoon orange emulco batter into outer ring.

7. Bake at 160°C for 15 minutes, then 140°C for 30 minutes.

8. Invert pan on a wire rack to cool completely before unmoulding.

Sakura Matcha Cake

Makes one 18-cm cake

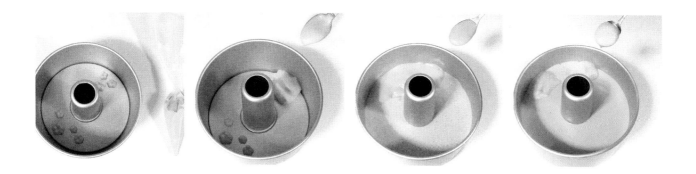

Egg yolk batter

3 egg yolks

25 g castor sugar

50 g vegetable/corn oil

50 g water/fresh milk

80 g cake flour, sifted

A pinch of salt

$\frac{1}{4}$ tsp strawberry paste

2 tsp matcha powder, sifted

Meringue

4 egg whites

$\frac{1}{4}$ tsp cream of tartar

45 g castor sugar

1. Prepare egg yolk batter (page 20). Spoon 6 tsp batter into a small bowl and add strawberry paste to get pink batter. Add matcha powder to remaining egg yolk batter and mix well for green batter.

2. Prepare meringue (page 20). Spoon 12 Tbsp meringue into another bowl and gently fold into pink batter one-third at a time. Gently fold remaining meringue into pink batter one-third at a time.

3. Spoon pink batter into a piping bag and cut a 3-mm hole at the tip. Pipe 5 dots per flower on base of chiffon tube pan. Ensure that dots are piped sufficiently thick so pattern will form nicely and not stick to base of chiffon pan when cake is unmoulded. Bake at 160°C for 1$\frac{1}{2}$ minutes. Set pan aside.

4. Fold remaining meringue into green batter one-third at a time. Spoon half the green batter gently over baked flowers.

5. Pipe or spoon remaining pink batter over green batter to create a thin pink layer, then repeat to spoon green batter into pan until batter is about 2 cm from rim of pan.

6. Bake at 160°C for 15 minutes, then 140°C for 30 minutes.

7. Invert pan on a wire rack to cool completely before unmoulding.

8. Using a fine-tipped brush, complete flowers by drawing pink dots in centre using $\frac{1}{2}$ tsp beetroot powder dissolved in 1 tsp hot water or a food marker.

Double Rainbow Cake

Makes one 15-cm cake

Egg yolk batter

3 egg yolks

20 g castor sugar

40 g vegetable/corn oil

37 g water

1 tsp vanilla extract

60 g cake flour, sifted

A pinch of salt

Pink, yellow, orange, blue, green and purple gel food colouring

Meringue

4 egg whites

1/4 tsp cream of tartar

45 g castor sugar

1. Preheat oven to 160°C. Prepare a 15-cm chiffon tube pan.

2. Prepare egg yolk batter (page 20). Spoon 3 tsp batter each into 6 small bowls. Add a different food colouring to each bowl to create rainbow colours. Leave remaining batter plain.

3. Prepare meringue (page 20). Gently fold 6 Tbsp meringue into each coloured batter one-third at a time.

4. Gently fold remaining meringue into plain batter one-third at a time.

5. Spoon coloured batters into separate piping bags and cut a 2 mm hole at the tip. Pipe concentric circles on base of chiffon pan, starting with purple at the centre of pan, then continuing with blue, green, orange and yellow. Place removable base back into pan and pipe last concentric circle in pink.

6. Bake at 160°C for 1 1/2 minutes.

7. Spoon plain batter over rainbow pattern. Bake at 160°C for 10 minutes, then 140°C for 10–12 minutes, or until a skewer inserted into the centre of cake comes out clean.

8. Invert pan on a wire rack to cool completely before unmoulding.

9. Unmould cake and slice in half to create double rainbows.

Airplane Cake

Makes one 23-cm cake

Recipe on pages 100 and 101

White vanilla chiffon

Egg yolk batter

1 egg yolk

27 g castor sugar

52 g vegetable/corn oil

49 g water

1½ tsp vanilla extract

80 g cake flour, sifted

A pinch of salt

Meringue

5 egg whites

¼ tsp cream of tartar

45 g castor sugar

1. Preheat oven to 160°C. Place a tray of water under the lowest rack in the oven for steam baking. Prepare a 23-cm airplane cake pan.

2. Prepare egg yolk batter (page 20) and meringue (page 20) for white vanilla chiffon.

3. Gently fold meringue into egg yolk batter one-third at a time.

4. Pour batter into airplane cake pan until batter is about 1.5 cm from rim of pan.

5. Bake at 160°C for 15 minutes, 150°C for 10 minutes, 140°C for 15 minutes and 130°C for 5–10 minutes, or until a skewer inserted into the centre of cake comes out clean.

6. Invert pan on a wire rack to cool completely before unmoulding.

7. Preheat oven to 160°C. Line a 23-cm square baking pan with baking paper.

8. Pour remaining white vanilla chiffon batter into baking tray and bake at 160°C for 14 minutes.

9. Invert sheet cake onto a sheet of baking paper and let cool.

Coloured sheet cakes

Egg yolk batter

2 egg yolks

13 g castor sugar

23 g vegetable/corn oil

25 g water

1 tsp vanilla extract

40 g cake flour, sifted

Blue, red and black
  gel food colouring

Meringue

3 egg whites

$1/_5$ tsp cream of tartar

30 g castor sugar

Finishing

Marshmallow cream (page 24)

Pink food marker (optional)

10. Line a 20-cm and a 25-cm square baking pan with baking paper.

11. Prepare egg yolk batter (page 20) for coloured sheet cakes. Spoon batter into 4 separate bowls: 8 tsp for blue, 6 tsp for red, 3 tsp for yellow and 3 tsp for black. Add a little of the respective food colouring and mix well.

12. Prepare meringue (page 20) for coloured sheet cakes. Gently fold meringue into each egg yolk batter one-third at a time: 16 Tbsp meringue into blue batter, 12 Tbsp meringue into red batter and 6 Tbsp meringue each into yellow and black batters.

13. Pour blue batter into prepared 20-cm pan and bake at 160°C for 14 minutes.

14. Pour red, yellow and black batters side by side into prepared 25-cm pan and bake at 160°C for 14 minutes.

15. Invert sheet cakes onto separate sheets of baking paper and let cool.

16. Peel baking paper from sheet cakes and place on cutting mats.

17. From blue sheet cake, use an oval cutter to cut an oval for airplane window. Use a knife to cut 2 thin strips and a trapezium for pattern on airplane and for rudder.

18. Use a star cutter to cut out 4 stars from red sheet cake to decorate airplane.

19. Use a round cutter to cut out a circle from yellow sheet cake. Use a knife to slice off 2 sides for pattern on airplane.

20. From white sheet cake, use a round cutter to cut out 4 circles to decorate airplane. Use a cloud or flower cutter to cut out 4–5 clouds. Use an oval cutter to cut out 2 ovals for white of eyes and a straw to cut out 2 small white circles for eyes.

21. Use a circle cutter to cut out mouth of airplane by making 2 cuts 1 mm apart on black sheet cake. Use a small round cutter to cut out 2 eye balls.

22. Adhere parts with marshmallow cream. Use a pink food marker to add rosy cheeks if desired.

Colourful Caterpillar Cake

Recipe on pages 104 and 105

Egg yolk batter

4 egg yolks

27 g castor sugar

53 g vegetable/corn oil

50 g water

1 1/2 tsp vanilla extract

80 g cake flour, sifted

A pinch of salt

Pink, yellow, orange, green, blue and purple gel food colouring

1/4 tsp charcoal powder

Meringue

5 egg whites

60 g castor sugar

1/4 tsp cream of tartar

Finishing

Marshmallow cream (page 24)

1. Preheat oven to 160°C. Prepare 6 round glass bowls, each 11-cm in diameter and a cake pop mould. Line a 15-cm square baking pan with baking paper.

2. Prepare egg yolk batter (page 20). Spoon 5 tsp batter each into 6 separate bowls. Add a different food colouring to each bowl and mix well.

3. Spoon 3 tsp batter into another bowl. Add charcoal powder and mix well.

4. Leave remaining batter plain.

5. Prepare meringue (page 20). Gently fold meringue into each egg yolk batter one-third at a time: 10 Tbsp meringue to each rainbow-coloured batter, 6 Tbsp to black batter and remainder to plain batter.

6. Spoon rainbow-coloured batters into separate glass bowls. Gently tap bowls on counter top to release any air bubbles. Bake at 160°C for 10 minutes, then 150°C for 20–23 minutes, or until a skewer inserted into the centre of cakes comes out clean.

7. Invert bowls on a wire rack to cool completely before unmoulding.

8. Preheat oven to 160°C. Spoon plain batter into 2 cavities of cake pop mould and bake for 12 minutes. Leave on a wire rack to cool completely before unmoulding.

9. Pour black batter and remaining plain batter into prepared 15-cm pan and bake at 160°C for 14 minutes.

10. Invert sheet cake onto a sheet of baking paper and let cool.

11. Peel baking paper from sheet cake and place on a cutting mat.

12. From black sheet cake, use an oval cutter to cut out 2 ovals for eyes. Use a large oval cutter to cut out mouth of caterpillar by making 2 cuts 1 mm apart. Repeat this step to make feelers by cutting the semi-circular strip in half. Use a large straw to cut out 2 circles for ends of feelers.

13. Use a large straw to cut out circles from plain cake to complete eyes.

14. Use a sharp knife to slice off two sides of yellow, orange, green and blue cakes to shape caterpillar's body. Slice only one side of pink and purple cakes for head and tail end of caterpillar.

15. Use a large straw to cut 2 circles from slice of pink cake for cheeks.

16. Adhere parts using marshmallow cream.

17. Cut cake pop into 8 segments using a sharp knife for caterpillar legs. Stick them to cake board using marshmallow cream.

Hidden Surprise Strawberry Cake

Makes one 17-cm heart-shaped cake

Vanilla sheet cake

Egg yolk batter

2 egg yolks

13 g castor sugar

23 g vegetable/corn oil

30 g water

40 g cake flour, sifted

A pinch of salt

1 tsp strawberry paste

Meringue

3 egg whites

$^{1}/_{5}$ tsp cream of tartar

30 g castor sugar

Strawberry chiffon

Egg yolk batter

3 egg yolks

20 g castor sugar

35 g vegetable/corn oil

45 g strawberry purée

60 g cake flour, sifted

1 tsp strawberry paste

Meringue

4 egg whites

$^{1}/_{4}$ tsp cream of tartar

45 g castor sugar

1. Preheat oven to 160°C. Line a 25-cm square baking pan with baking paper.

2. Prepare egg yolk batter (page 20) for vanilla sheet cake. Add strawberry paste and mix well.

3. Prepare meringue (page 20) for vanilla sheet cake. Gently fold meringue into egg yolk batter one-third at a time.

4. Pour batter into prepared pan. Gently tap pan on counter top to release any air bubbles. Bake at 160°C for 14 minutes.

5. Invert sheet cake onto a sheet of baking sheet and let cool.

6. Peel baking paper from sheet cake and place on a cutting mat. Use a small heart cutter to cut a small heart, a medium heart cutter to cut a medium heart and a large heart cutter to cut out a large heart. Repeat to use the large heart cutter to cut out as many hearts as you can from rest of sheet cake.

7. Preheat oven to 160°C. Prepare a 17-cm heart-shape chiffon tube pan.

8. Prepare egg yolk batter (page 20) and meringue (page 20) for strawberry chiffon. Gently fold meringue into egg yolk batter one-third at a time.

9. Arrange small, medium and a large heart on the top left corner of pan. Gently spoon a layer of batter over to cover hearts, until layer is about 2-cm thick.

10. Arrange remaining hearts, pointed side up, in a ring in pan. Line them up closely. Pour remaining batter over to cover ring of hearts.

11. Bake at 160°C for 15 minutes, then 140°C for 30 minutes, or until a skewer inserted into the centre of cake comes out clean.

12. Invert pan on a wire rack to cool completely before unmoulding.

Matcha Azuki Hidden Hearts Roll Cake

Makes one 25-cm roll cake

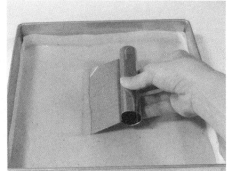

Recipe on pages 110 and 111

White chocolate ganache

185 g whipping cream
60 g white chocolate, chopped
A pinch of salt
100 g chunky azuki bean paste

Azuki sheet cake

Egg yolk batter

2 egg yolks
10 g castor sugar
28 g vegetable/corn oil
30 g smooth azuki bean paste
$1/4$ tsp vanilla extract
35 g cake flour, sifted
A pinch of salt
$1/8$ tsp red liquid food colouring

Meringue

3 egg whites
$1/5$ tsp cream of tartar
30 g castor sugar

1. Prepare white chocolate ganache a day ahead. Heat cream in a small saucepan until bubbles start to appear. Remove from heat and pour over white chocolate in a heatproof bowl. Stir until white chocolate is melted. Add salt and stir to dissolve.

2. Place bowl in an ice bath and stir until mixture is cool. Cover and refrigerate overnight to chill.

3. Prepare azuki sheet cake. Preheat oven to 160°C. Line a 25-cm square baking pan with baking paper.

4. Prepare egg yolk batter (page 20) for azuki chiffon. Add red colouring and mix well.

5. Prepare meringue (page 20) for azuki chiffon. Gently fold meringue into egg yolk batter one-third at a time.

6. Pour batter into prepared baking pan. Use a pastry scraper to level batter. Gently tap pan on counter top to release any air bubbles.

7. Bake sheet cake at 160°C for 14 minutes, or until skewer inserted into the centre of cake comes out clean. Invert cake onto a sheet of baking paper and let cool.

8. Peel baking paper from sheet cake and place on a cutting mat. Use a heart shape cutter to cut out enough hearts to line length of roll cake when stacked together.

9. Use marshmallow cream to stick hearts together. Cover with plastic wrap and place in an airtight container until ready to assemble.

Matcha chiffon

Egg yolk batter

2 egg yolks

10 g castor sugar

28 g vegetable/corn oil

25 g matcha paste (made by mixing 2 tsp matcha powder and 25 g hot water, then strained and cooled)

$1/2$ tsp vanilla extract

40 g cake flour, sifted

A pinch of salt

Meringue

3 egg whites

$1/5$ tsp cream of tartar

35 g castor sugar

Finishing

Marshmallow cream (page 24)

Syrup (page 24)

10. Prepare matcha chiffon. Preheat oven to 160°C. Line a 25-cm square baking pan with baking paper.

11. Prepare egg yolk batter (page 20) and meringue (page 20) for matcha chiffon. Gently fold meringue into egg yolk batter one-third at a time.

12. Pour batter into prepared pan and use a pastry scraper to level batter. Gently tap tray on counter top to release any air bubbles.

13. Bake at 160°C for 14 minutes, or until a skewer inserted into the centre of cake comes out clean.

14. Invert cake onto a sheet of baking paper and roll up. Set aside to cool in rolled up position to prevent cake from cracking when cooled.

15. Remove white chocolate ganache from refrigerator. Place bowl in an ice bath and whisk to stiff peaks. Be careful not to over beat.

16. Measure out 30 g whipped ganache in a bowl and add chunky azuki bean paste. Mix well.

17. Unroll cooled matcha chiffon and brush surface with syrup. Spread with a layer of azuki-white chocolate ganache, then top with a layer of white chocolate ganache.

18. Arrange row of hearts, pointed side up, in a row in the middle of cake.

19. Roll cake up to enclose hearts, using baking paper to shape and tighten roll to ensure cream gets into the crevices of hearts. Refrigerate until ganache is set.

20. Use a serrated knife to trim ends of roll to neaten, cleaning the knife after each cut. Serve chilled.

Weights & Measures

Quantities for this book are given in Metric and American spoon measures.
Standard spoon measurements used are: 1 teaspoon = 5 ml and 1 tablespoon = 15 ml.
All measures are level unless otherwise stated.

LIQUID AND VOLUME MEASURES

Metric	Imperial	American
5 ml	1/6 fl oz	1 teaspoon
10 ml	1/3 fl oz	1 dessertspoon
15 ml	1/2 fl oz	1 tablespoon
60 ml	2 fl oz	1/4 cup (4 tablespoons)
85 ml	2 1/2 fl oz	1/3 cup
90 ml	3 fl oz	3/8 cup (6 tablespoons)
125 ml	4 fl oz	1/2 cup
180 ml	6 fl oz	3/4 cup
250 ml	8 fl oz	1 cup
300 ml	10 fl oz (1/2 pint)	1 1/4 cups
375 ml	12 fl oz	1 1/2 cups
435 ml	14 fl oz	1 3/4 cups
500 ml	16 fl oz	2 cups
625 ml	20 fl oz (1 pint)	2 1/2 cups
750 ml	24 fl oz (1 1/5 pints)	3 cups
1 litre	32 fl oz (1 3/5 pints)	4 cups
1.25 litres	40 fl oz (2 pints)	5 cups
1.5 litres	48 fl oz (2 2/5 pints)	6 cups
2.5 litres	80 fl oz (4 pints)	10 cups

OVEN TEMPERATURE

	°C	°F	Gas Regulo
Very slow	120	250	1
Slow	150	300	2
Moderately slow	160	325	3
Moderate	180	350	4
Moderately hot	190/200	370/400	5/6
Hot	210/220	410/440	6/7
Very hot	230	450	8
Super hot	250/290	475/550	9/10

DRY MEASURES

Metric	Imperial
30 grams	1 ounce
45 grams	1 1/2 ounces
55 grams	2 ounces
70 grams	2 1/2 ounces
85 grams	3 ounces
100 grams	3 1/2 ounces
110 grams	4 ounces
125 grams	4 1/2 ounces
140 grams	5 ounces
280 grams	10 ounces
450 grams	16 ounces (1 pound)
500 grams	1 pound, 1 1/2 ounces
700 grams	1 1/2 pounds
800 grams	1 3/4 pounds
1 kilogram	2 pounds, 3 ounces
1.5 kilograms	3 pounds, 4 1/2 ounces
2 kilograms	4 pounds, 6 ounces

LENGTH

Metric	Imperial
0.5 cm	1/4 inch
1 cm	1/2 inch
1.5 cm	3/4 inch
2.5 cm	1 inch

ABBREVIATION

tsp	teaspoon
Tbsp	tablespoon
g	gram
kg	kilogram
ml	millilitre